DATE DUE			
AUG 2 8 1993	FEB 0 7 1997	JAN 1 3 2001	
SEP 0 6 1993	AUG 2 2 1997	APR 2 5 2001	
SEP 1 0 1993	JAN 1 0 1998	DEC 2 6 2001	
OCT 0 4 1993	MAR 3 0 199	MAY 2003 2004	
OCT 3 0 1993	APR 2 2 1998	AUG 1 9 2004	
FEB 2 3 1994	JUL 2 2 1998		
MAY 1 8 1994	AUG 7 1998		
NOV 2 5 1994	MAR 0 1999		
JAN 1 7 1995	JUN 1 7 1999		
APR 1 7 1995	FEB 1 5 2000		
JUN 2 0 1995	JUL 1 0 2000		
MAY 0 2 1996			

Christopher Lloyd's FLOWER GARDEN

Christopher Lloyd's
FLOWER GARDEN

Photography by
Steven Wooster

DORLING KINDERSLEY
London • New York • Stuttgart

A DORLING KINDERSLEY BOOK

Created, designed and edited by Steven Wooster and Susan Berry, 47 Crewys Road, Childs Hill, London NW2 2AU
Still life photography by Sue Atkinson, Arc Studios

First American Edition, 1993

2 4 6 8 10 9 7 5 3 1

Published in the United States by
Dorling Kindersley, Inc., 232 Madison Avenue
New York, New York 10016

Lloyd, Christopher, 1921 –
  [Flower garden]
  Christopher Lloyd's flower garden. — 1st American ed.
  p. cm.
  Includes index.
  ISBN 1–56458–167–5
  1. Great Dixter Gardens (England) 2. Flower gardening —England—
East Sussex. 3. Plants, Ornamental —England—East Sussex.
I. Title. II. Title: Flower garden.
SB466.G8G742 1993   92–53449
712—dc20   CIP

Typesetting by SX Composing Limited, Great Britain

Reproduced by Colourscan, Singapore

Printed and bound in Singapore by Star Standard Industries.

CONTENTS

Preface

THE PAGES that follow describe many aspects of my garden in fair detail, but "What and where is this garden?" and "Who is Christopher Lloyd?" are questions that deserve answers.

Great Dixter is a fifteenth-century, half-timbered manor house in the Weald of Sussex (and Kent). It had been on the market for ten years when my parents were house hunting, in 1910, and first saw it. They had married in 1905 and lived in London. My father was a color printer in Blackfriars, where he had founded his own firm, Nathaniel Lloyd & Co. It must have prospered because he was able to give it up on moving permanently to Great Dixter in 1912.

He engaged Edwin Lutyens to restore and add to the house, and to design the garden. It was a good relationship with happy results. The Sunk Garden, not made until after the First World War, was my father's design. My mother was a passionate gardener (when she wasn't making clothes for her husband and family of six, or cooking or whatever – her hands were never idle) so it was a pretty effective team. It was also a good background to be brought up in. I was the youngest of six and loved plants right from the start. Fortunately, none of the other members of my family were a bit interested – competition always leads to arguments.

I was born at Dixter (in 1921) and, with gaps for education and the War, have lived there all my life. Education included a spell of seven years (1947-54) at Wye College, University of London, where I first took a degree, and then became an assistant lecturer in what would now be called amenity horticulture (I hate that word, amenity, with its connotation of doling out leisure to the masses). Thank goodness there was far more practical horticulture taught at Wye in those days than now, so that what with my home base and what Wye taught me, my grounding wasn't too bad, although at the time I was teaching I was only one step ahead of the students.

Not many people can live at a place like Dixter and simultaneously earn a living. When I returned for good in 1954, that was what I had to do. I started a nursery for less usual plants (plants I enjoy growing myself; I've never been good at selling what I don't believe in). By intention, that has always remained a small concern as I wanted it to be personal, and there's not much fun in a huge business where you can't keep your finger on every pulse (although Beth Chatto seems to manage with hers, I must admit). The house and gardens are open to the public on six afternoons a week from April to October (my brother, Quentin, runs this enterprise), so it was natural for visitors to want plants they had seen.

As a source of income, my writings became of far greater importance, however. I submitted my first article to *Gardening Illustrated* in 1952. In 1957, my first book, *The Mixed Border*, was published. I was disappointed that so little notice was taken of it, but who was Christopher Lloyd anyway? I plugged on, largely because I love the English language and writing in it is its own reward. And I love to communicate the joy that plants and gardening give me.

So there it is. I spend too much time writing and too little actually gardening. But my best and most immediate writing is done when I have become excited by what I've just been doing in the garden (or so I like to think). You need the balance and it has worked out pretty well, especially as I have the benefit of so many stimulating friends around me, many of them first met as customers or visitors to the garden. Weekends at Dixter are pretty lively. I think of these times as my Indian summer.

Christopher Lloyd –

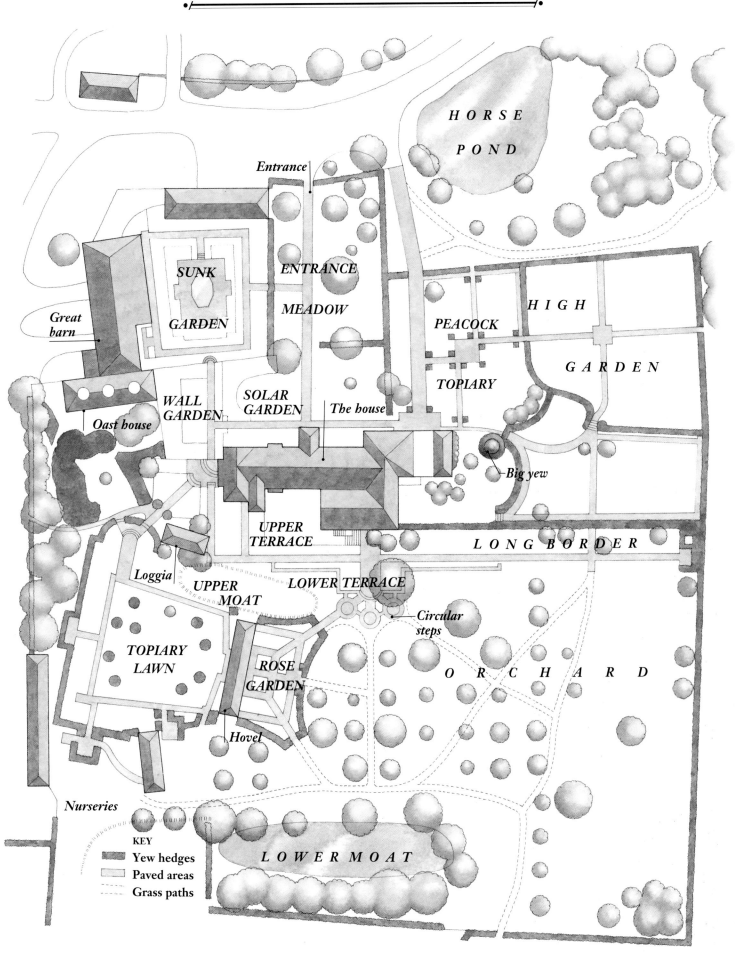

HORSE
POND

Entrance

ENTRANCE

MEADOW

HIGH

PEACOCK

GARDEN

Great
barn

TOPIARY

SUNK

GARDEN

WALL
GARDEN

SOLAR
GARDEN

The house

Oast house

Big yew

UPPER
TERRACE

LONG BORDER

Loggia

LOWER TERRACE

UPPER
MOAT

Circular
steps

TOPIARY
LAWN

ROSE
GARDEN

O R C H A R D

Hovel

Nurseries

KEY

Yew hedges

Paved areas

Grass paths

L O W E R   M O A T

SPRING

Still lots of bare earth in spring, but increasingly masked, especially with me, by forget-me-nots (Myositis), here joined by bluebells, cranesbills, and Welsh poppies. There is a range of willows, bearing pussy catkins, such as those of Salix hastata 'Wehrhahni', not forgetting the swooning scent of Osmanthus delavayi.

Spring flowers

THERE IS NO spring garden, as such, at Dixter. The meadows are lively. Bedding is, for the most part, integrated into mixed borders. And there are spring underplantings to later features. I believe in keeping my eye focused on summer and autumn. There are plenty of spring incidents, but my object is to include them in such a way that they do not detract with gaps or general slovenliness from the later summer or autumn scene.

Rheum palmatum, with young purple rhubarb leaves, particularly persistent on their undersides, and a great panicle of white flowers (in the form I had from the Savill Gardens at Windsor) looks good against a dark background. It is at the back of a wide border because I know that it will die off quite early in the summer, but there are herbaceous plants in front of it that will by then be masking the gap.

Here, also in the Barn Garden, are two spring-flowering spurges. *Euphorbia palustris*, the taller, is lime-green and combines well with 'White Triumphator' tulips. It is in a damp, cool border. The shorter *E. polychroma* is a bright shade of yellow, though not so long-lasting. There is something of a yellow and white theme around here with, additionally,

Partners
Two plants (above) that look good together in my Rose Garden are the late-flowering, pale yellow hyacinth, 'City of Haarlem', around a perennial pea, Lathyrus vernus. They contrast in habit, color and flower form, but without in any way shouting the odds.

●

Ornamental rhubarb
Rheum palmatum *(left) has rather jagged leaves, which are often colored when young, especially on their undersides; sometimes reddish, sometimes, as here, purple-red. The flowers may be pink, but are white in this clone, and I think they contrast well with their foliage.*

———●———

In cottage-garden style
This jumble of spring flowerers (right) includes the pale yellow spikes of a pea flower, Thermopsis; a dwarf Jacob's-ladder, Polemonium 'Lambrook Mauve', at the front; some yellow Welsh poppies; a giant bluebell; and the magenta 'Bevan's Variety' of the cranesbill, Geranium macrorrhizum.

Brides wear white
Exochorda × macrantha *'The Bride'* (left) surprised me by growing taller than I expected. It is easily controlled, however, by hard pruning immediately after flowering. Not to weaken it excessively, I do this only in alternate years. Vigorous young growth is made during the summer, and it flowers the following spring.

—— • ——

Hummocky spurge
As bright a yellow (with the minimum of green) as any spurge is Euphorbia polychroma *(right). Its habit is neat and hummocky. I like to contrast this with red anemones. Between the clumps you see the developing gray foliage of Lychnis coronaria.*

—— • ——

Aggressive but nice
Welsh poppies, Meconopsis cambrica *(below), sow themselves everywhere and are especially luxuriant where the root run is cool. We have both the yellow and the orange forms, yellow being commonest in the wild.*

the small, double white *Prunus glandulosa* 'Alba Plena', *Exochorda × macrantha* 'The Bride', as well as a yellow, May-flowering jonquil, *Narcissus* 'Tittle Tattle'. Briefly and excitingly, they are joined late in April by the hardy *Arum creticum* in its yellow-flowered form. Around the corner, in a south-facing border, is a low, shrubby pea, *Coronilla valentina*. It smothers itself in warmly scented yellow blossom. You never quite know when this bush will start flowering; sometimes it is in October and continuing right through the winter, but sometimes not until well into spring. I should like to surround it with blue *Scilla siberica*, which flowers in March, but the chances are they wouldn't coincide.

However, I do have a carpet of this scilla nearby in a mainly summer-flowering bed, close enough to be admired.

On the Barn Garden's south side there is a colony of the dwarf almond, *Prunus tenella*, wreathed in pink blossom in April. It is never more than 15in (38cm) tall, because I prune it hard after flowering. This is interplanted with snowdrops and with *Arabis caucasica* 'Flore Pleno', whose double white rosettes look charming under the pink. There is a double red *Camellia japonica* 'Margherita Coleoni' in one corner, and this is underplanted with the deep blue *Omphalodes cappadocica*, which will stand a great deal of shade. The Wall Garden does not have many unusual spring features, besides ferns, tulips, periwinkles,

Bergenia purpurascens, with rich purple flowers, and notably *Epimedium pinnatum* 'Colchicum'. There is coppery young foliage on this ground-cover perennial, creating a foil for its sprays of bright yellow flowers. To set it off, I have planted a patch behind of *Narcissus* 'Liberty Bells', a Triandrus hybrid with lemon-yellow flowers.

Through the archway and down the steps, there is a spring planting with a clump of the bold bluebell, 'Chevithorn', a dwarf, clumpy Jacob's ladder, 'Lambrook Mauve', and a pale yellow *Thermopsis*, with spikes of pea flowers. Welsh poppies are scattered around and the lime-green young shoots of a hemerocallis also make a contribution.

A big gap in the ilex hedge (*Quercus ilex*, an evergreen oak), here, needs explaining. Two units in it were killed through my allowing a huge rambler rose, and an ivy, to engulf them. When all was cleared away, the twisted stems of an old ornamental crab, *Malus floribunda*, were revealed. Planted when the garden was first made, the best view of it in flower is from the front of the house, seen over the top of the Wall Garden

wall. Its trunks are so beautifully formed that I have decided, for the time being, to leave the gap, which I have planted with low ground cover: more *Epimedium pinnatum* 'Colchicum' and a blue lungwort, *Pulmonaria* 'Lewis Palmer'.

I love hyacinths; their waxy stiffness, the squeak of their foliage and, above all, their scent. So I have them in succession, indoors and out, often picking the outside ones to bring in, from late January (I can't abide those specially treated to flower at Christmas) to early May. Those that have flowered in bowls are saved and planted out to do another turn. One early effect that has resulted in a warm border on the lower terrace, traditionally doing its stuff late in March, has a

Welcome interloper
It was the lime-green Smyrnium perfoliatum*'s own idea to sow itself into this picture (opposite), which officially comprises the amazing Viridiflora tulip 'Hollywood' and the neat-leaved* Bergenia purpurascens – *late flowering, tall, and very free. The whorled foliage of* Lilium martagon *gives promise of blossom in June.*

•

Double primroses
I'm not very good with double primroses (left), which often go down with virus diseases and always seem to be fading out – at least with me, though some gardeners make them their life's hobby. The double white one is just a double white; the powder-blue variety is 'Bronwyn'.

GROWING
Scillas

The scilla shown here is the early-, March-flowering *Scilla bifolia*, which I have combined with stupefying panache with the young, lime-green foliage of *Valeriana phu* 'Aurea'. A shame there's no one around at the time to admire my brilliance. Actually, this scilla is a lot bluer than it looks here. The better-known *S. siberica* is bluer still, rather late flowering, and it covers a remarkably long season, throwing up a succession of flower spikes from each bulb. 'Spring Beauty' is exactly the same.

Spring themes
Forget-me-nots are a theme running through many of my borders in spring. So are Welsh poppies. The different color forms of honesty or money flower, Lunaria annua, *I try to assign to special locations, so that they do not interbreed. Here is the white one (above). The sharply defined, variegated foliage in the foreground belongs to a comfrey,* Symphytum × uplandicum.

white Cynthella hyacinth (bred to be less big and muscular than the standard types) among clumps of the 4in- (10cm-) tall, tiny, yellow trumpet daffodil, *Narcissus minor*. Another team that seems to me to work well, though it is a bit unconventional, is a pale pink hyacinth in front of *Spiraea japonica* 'Goldflame', whose coppery young foliage soon changes to pale yellow.

Another pink and yellow perpetration that I achieve in May is at the flowering of pink *Deutzia* x *rosea*, with the self-sowing yellow and white annual, *Limnanthes douglasii*, in front of it. Towards the end of its flowering period, this combination is joined by a light blue Dutch iris.

— *Towards spring's end* —

The Long Border is waking up throughout May, and not just thanks to the tulips. A patch of sea kale at the border's front carries mounds of white, honey-scented blossom. Behind it is some of the magenta *Gladiolus byzantinus*, which makes itself comfortable in many parts of the garden and is rarely in the way; its dying remains don't flop around, like daffodils, but are easily absorbed. A little beyond, it grows through *Euonymus* x *fortunei* 'Silver Queen', which would be hard to beat for year-round beauty, but is now outstandingly fresh, with pale yellow margins to its young leaves.

Near to the cross path, the stiff, tawny orange spears of *Libertia peregrinans* combine not only with forget-me-nots but also with the stately spikes of blue stars in bold clumps of *Camassia leichtlinii* 'Electra'. More stars appear at the back along the blush-white spikes of the 8ft (2.3m) tall foxtail lily, *Eremurus robustus*. There are clumps of these either side of the yew archway, but for some reason one of them always seems to do better than the other.

In the High Garden there has been an accidental triumph, enjoyed right at spring's end, where a Portugal broom, *Cytisus albus*, seeded itself tight up against the base of a yew hedge. Its wands of small, white, pea-like flowers are well served by the dark yew background. These brooms are not long-lived, but their life can be doubled by regular pruning away of all the flowered shoots as soon as the display is past. This I have regularly done and the bush, some 7ft (2m) tall, is six or seven years old by now but cannot, I fear, last much longer. There are rich crimson double peonies in front of it, and a froth of

Catch them early, catch them young
March needs to go out like a lamb to give some of these flowers (below) their chance. Narcissus 'Aflame' is perhaps even better for picking than it is grown in the garden, where the brilliance of its cup soon bleaches. Wild primroses are in front.

Double act P.87

You can compare this spring scene (right) with the same area in June (page 89), when the background elder is flowering. White trumpet Narcissus 'Cantatrice' is my favorite among these daffodils, which are planted among Hybrid Musk 'Penelope' roses. Interplanting roses with bulbs is a good idea, as it provides spring interest, apart from the small drawback that feeding the roses, which they like, is inclined to make the narcissi grow too flimsy and weak-stemmed.

Primaries for contrast

The juxtaposition of primary colors, such as blue and yellow (below), makes for strong contrast. If each of the colors is itself strong, the eye will quickly tire, especially beneath the blazing sun of midsummer. But here are two flowers of early spring when we are starved of color, and we are delighted to be distracted. The double Queen Anne's jonquil is a very old narcissus and it is not a bit assertive. Bright blue Scilla siberica flowers all around it.

London pride, *Saxifraga umbrosa*. These, as infillers, have quite an extended range, and I like them most where they combine with the young purple-bronze foliage of *Rodgersia pinnata* 'Superba' and the pale gray of a low-growing bush willow, *Salix helvetica*. The paths in the High Garden are in the form of a cross and if you take the arm leading to the oak gate, which itself takes you out to the freedom of the Horse Pond area, a wonderful gust of sweet almondy scent will rise to envelop you, especially if the wind is from the north, which it so often is in May. This scent comes from the multitude of tiny greenish buff blossoms on a large, lumpy shrub (*Elaeagnus umbellata*) established on the bank overlooking the pond.

There is not a wealth of spring blossom from the trees at Dixter. For one thing, the yew hedges made it unnecessary and undesirable to plant many trees within their compartments. For another, bullfinches make such a mess of many spring flowerers. Lastly, I consider that most flowering crabs, cherries, and other prunus make pretty dull viewing through the summer, and I don't encourage that kind of heaviness. But I do have a soft spot for hawthorns, and they make shapely trees. The large, double *Crataegus laevigata* 'Paul's Scarlet' near the Rose Garden was one of my own grafting on a volunteer seedling of wild hawthorn that occurred in the Rose Garden. And next to it is another of my own propagating, *C. persimilis* 'Prunifolia', with white blossom in May, followed by good autumn color in most years and deep red haws.

Plants in an architectural setting

IXTER'S GARDENS have a lot of bone structure. In fact, judging by photographs from the early days, they were severely skeletal. To a plantsman like me, this has been a boon. Left to myself, I might have found it hard to summon the discipline that every garden needs, no matter how high the plants for their own sakes stand in our schedule of priorities. Without a proper underlying structure, a garden can so easily dissolve into what turns out to be a seasonally charming but, in the final analysis, dissatisfying cottagey mess.

Our hardware consists of the house itself, which stands centrally with the garden all around it; nineteenth- or perhaps eighteenth-century farm buildings which Lutyens integrated into his designs; terraces in brick and stone; Yorkstone paving and steps; walls and formal, castellated yew hedges. The plantings themselves are sometimes formalized but on the whole they bring a smile to an otherwise severe face.

Formalized plantings are exemplified by espalier (and cordon) pears. My father had a passion for this fruit, and planted a number of pear trees at Dixter. They are now old and gnarled and covered with lichens (we no longer give them a winter spray of tar oil), while clematis have the cheek to scramble over them, but the intention is still clear. Visitors are particularly impressed by the venerable old pear tree whose fishbone structure climbs high against a huge chimney breast on the house's northwest end. They would like to be told that the tree bears delicious fruit, whereas the unfortunate reality is that the pear is a cooker of no interest, to me at any rate, though my dogs take great delight in gathering and crunching up the fallen crop in the autumn.

House and Wall Garden
*A border (right) with self-sowing
opium poppies and campanulas of
flimsy structure, but strengthened by
the setting and by the foliage of hostas
and veratrums. This is the solar wing
of the original 15th-century
half-timbered house.*

•

Wild pear in hedge
*The pear (left below), whose tiny
fruits are useless except to the birds,
was a feature before the gardens were
constructed and planted in 1910-1912.
Originally trimmed as a cone-shaped
topiary specimen, it was later
allowed to grow naturally. The yew
hedge was planted around it.*

Willow, elm, and yew
*A foliage feature in the Long Border
comprises these three species (above):
Dickson's golden elm, silver pollarded
willows and a yew hedge.*

—— *Accentuating the architecture* ——

The High Garden's layout is one that was fashionable in Edwardian times. Essential vegetable plots were concealed from view by, in this case, lines of espalier 'Comice' pears. In front of them, flower borders ran either side of straight flagstone paths, making a formal cross. Hence, in walking through this garden, you didn't need to be aware of the presence of mundane, utilitarian vegetables at all.

Where the paths crossed, the paving was extended into a square, which seemed to require the use of more important plants. Originally these were all of one hortensia hydrangea, 'Mme. A. Riverain'. Much as I love this flower, my affections are not all-inclusive. This one, in our soil, was a pale, washed-out pink or pinky mauve color. A garden boy carried cans around to water them every day in high summer, as he did the Lutyens-designed hydrangea tubs set in the lawns. I still see the point of growing some fairly heavy pieces around this central area, though they not infrequently change their identity and all are different. Five of these are conifers (they have to be renewed, from time to time) and so I call it conifer corner (there is a photograph of it on page 60).

Another example of plants accentuating the architectural nature of the setting is the figs that were planted in two places: one against the high barn wall in the Barn Garden, and the other against the brick wall dividing the upper and lower terraces on the house's southwest side. Their purpose was entirely to create a boldly handsome foliar effect. With this purpose in mind, the variety 'Brunswick' was chosen, its large leaves having more indentations than most.

In suitable years (perhaps one in four) this variety also carries the largest fruits of any fig I've met. Keeping a fig close into a wall, as can be seen against the National Gallery in Trafalgar Square, requires heavy annual pruning. However, as the fruit is borne only at the tips of the previous year's shoots, the less you prune, the greater are your chances of a crop. I am passionate about figs and, as a result, I consider it well worth the time and effort to protect a good crop from birds and wasps. And I am fairly lax on the pruning, which we normally carry out only one year in three.

As you enter the Barn Garden from the Wall Garden, the first feature that meets your eyes as you look across the Barn Garden is the tapestry of fig foliage. In between is a border, close to you, then the Sunk Garden with its octagonal pool, then more borders before the barn. Wherever you stand in this quadrilateral area, framed by two buildings, a wall, and a hedge, you see plants not only on the near side of the border close to you, but on the back side of borders viewed across the Sunk Garden. In practice, this means that the borders have to be planted with a view to being seen from both sides, but they are never without a background, as island beds all too often are, to their visual detriment.

Everyone gets the feeling, in this garden, of its being a complete entity, even though there has to be a backup area wherewith to keep it well furnished. The plantings are varied and detailed, but the firm structure holds it together. And, of course, I do use some bold plants, notably the big grasses, which help on the structural side.

— Softening effects —

The brick and tile archways at either end of the Wall Garden have Moresque intimations, reflected in the steps and paving beneath them, but are typically Lutyens. In spring, I like the way the arch leading from Wall to Barn Garden makes a background for the large colony of *Euphorbia griffithii* 'Fireglow'. This softens the severity of the architecture, which in turn stiffens what, by itself, could appear to be a formless froth.

That's not quite fair, because euphorbias always have a firm and characteristic design of their own. You see this again, going through the other archway, from the Wall Garden, towards the south terraces or, better still, looking upward from them towards the archway. The semicircular steps here have been colonized, either side of your passageway, by *Euphorbia amygdaloides robbiae*. They are volunteers and, in

Barn Garden corner
The large, rounded bush (above) is Osmanthus delavayi, *a semi-sculptural feature in this formally constructed garden, where there are altogether four such specimens, one on each corner of a quadrilateral. After their flowering, when they are smothered in heavily fragrant white blossom, they are immediately clipped. This has the additional advantage of stimulating a mass of young shoots in the ensuing summer season, and it is along these that the next spring's flowers are borne.*

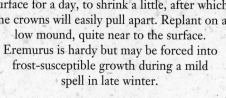

DIVIDING
Foxtail lilies

This foxtail lily, *Eremurus robustus*, rises quickly to 8ft (2.4m) at its flowering. Afterwards, it soon dies away, and I try to cover the spot with self-sowing nasturtiums. Its fleshy roots radiate starfishwise, quite near the surface, from a central crown. This may multiply by fission from time to time and can then be divided when the plant is quite dormant, in August. The roots are brittle and easily snapped. Each needs to be exposed, individually, till the entire plant can be lifted intact. Then leave it on the surface for a day, to shrink a little, after which the crowns will easily pull apart. Replant on a low mound, quite near to the surface. Eremurus is hardy but may be forced into frost-susceptible growth during a mild spell in late winter.

that sense, informal, yet they have a certain formality in their rosettes of dark, evergreen foliage, lightened in spring by pale green candelabrums. They provide a useful semi-structural feature by virtue of keeping their leaves in winter.

The lower terrace wall is boldly furnished by the fig against it, but is softened by an enormous *Magnolia* x *soulangeana* 'Lennei' to its right. This magnolia has an exceptionally flexible, floppy branch system. Tying it here and there to a back wall stiffens it helpfully. Its great pink goblets project like lamps, but, as to the space it takes up, I give it great latitude. Some branches come right down to the ground, and there you can look down into their goblets as a change from looking up at them. It seems to me to be the perfect complement to masonry, diluting its formality yet adding its own distinctive style. I discuss growing magnolias in greater detail in the chapter on structural shrubs on pages 60-63.

— *Mexican charmer* —

Where the magnolia spread-eagles onto paving, there is a recess with a narrow border (against the house) behind it. This contained spring and summer bedding, when I first knew it. For 40 years now, it has been occupied by the Mexican orange, *Choisya ternata*, boldly handsome at every season with its glossy, ternate, evergreen leaves. There comes a rush of scented white blossom in May and again, if the summer was hot, a good flowering in the autumn. However, my plant has spread much too far forward onto the paved area so, just

An early feature

To one side of the front path (above) stands a large bay laurel, Laurus nobilis, *which was already well established before the Lloyds arrived at Dixter in 1910. Its warm green coloring looks particularly cheerful in winter sunlight. Heavy snowfall splays its branches outward picturesquely, but severe frosts sometimes kill large portions back to a central core. It always recovers. This is a male tree that is covered with creamy blossom in May, scenting the air.*

A sculptural planting

Curved yew hedges converge (right) on an archway and a massive topiary specimen, originally a free-growing tree until my father cut it back and retrained it into a formal outline. With box hedging in the foreground and buildings behind, all is architectural. I have reduced incipient severity by planting an airy, bright green bamboo, Phyllostachys nigra, *in a key frontal position.*

before starting this book and after consultation with my gardening friends, we cut it more than halfway back. The next step will be to remove a paving stone in front of it and plant there the boldly architectural evergreen *Eryngium decaisneanum* (syn *E. pandanifolium*), with sea-green, scimitar leaves. It flowers in autumn with tall candelabrums – not colorful but full of character. In the center of the Long Border, it is lost. Here, on the contrary, it will stand out.

— *Terrace features* —

Lutyens's circular steps are nearby, leading down into the orchard meadow with just a strip of mown grass between. Moon daisies, *Leucanthemum vulgare* (hitherto *Chrysanthemum leucanthemum*), are a great May-June feature in the rough grass, and they have spread up into paving cracks on the steps. I like this link. The daisies have also invaded the upper terrace, where we sit out, as described in my chapter on self-sowers (see pages 80-85).

At the bottom of the lower terrace wall (plastered with aubrieta), where it overlooks the drained moat, there used to be an elm. That must have gone quite early; I never knew it. But I felt that a feature was needed here, preferably a vertical one. In 1956, while in Italy, I collected seed of a fastigiate cypress, *Cupressus sempervirens*, and I planted one of the resulting seedlings in this key spot. It was a good feature for the next 30 years, but then became long in the tooth, so I got rid of it. On the advice of a friend who knows his conifers better than anyone else I've met, I have replaced it with *Pinus strobus* 'Fastigiatus', which would, he said, remain better furnished the length of its stem than the fastigiate form of Scots pine. It is not a common plant and the nurseryman I applied to kindly grafted one specially for me, so it was quite tiny when I received it six months later, but I am not impatient in that sort of way. It is still very small but growing lustily, so I am happy.

— *Backgrounds for borders* —

The Long Border, which is 15ft (4.8m) deep from front to back, has a yew hedge behind it along its entire length. What a boon that is for setting off its contents. When people extol island beds, pointing out, truly, that the plants in them do not get drawn and weak in the stem as in one-sided borders (where there is darkness on one side), they forget about the importance of backgrounds and how seldom these are provided in the context of an island bed.

The Sunk Garden

The sunken area within the Barn Garden (left) was designed and created by my father, Nathaniel, after the First World War, on what had, in the original design, been a lawn. The pool is octagonal, but with two of its opposite sides longer than the other six. The paved area around it is softened by plants, some of them self-sowing – for example, England's native spotted orchid, whose dust-fine seed blew in on the wind.

Leading through

I particularly like the orange of Euphorbia griffithii *'Fireglow' (left), against the brickwork of the wall, and the archway leading to the Barn Garden. This is a spring scene, but the euphorbia continues throughout the summer. For winter, when the ground is bare, I have planted bulbs of the dwarf blue* Iris histrioides *'Major', which flowers very early in the year, in the gaps between the euphorbia's rhizomes.*

Self-appointed

It is not always easy to find the most effective position to display the wand flower's graces, but this plant of Dierama pulcherrimum *(right) was a self-sown seedling that placed itself ideally, at the top end of one of the Michaelmas daisy hedges that link topiary 'peacocks' in this part of the garden. It is a South African plant that is reasonably hardy given good drainage.*

Generally we want lots of color in our beds and borders, but without dark or at least somber backgrounds the color is never highlighted. If the island bed is large enough so that you are not even aware that it is an island, you can plant large, informal shrubs like laurustinus (*Viburnum tinus*) or the wrinkle-leaved *V. rhytidophyllum* in the center of it. Informal though they are, they will provide excellent backgrounds for the lower level of planting. But small island beds of perennials look almost as self-conscious and uncomfortable as bedding-out beds do in all but the most formal contexts.

My Dickson's golden elm, *Ulmus* 'Dampieri Aurea', looks excellent with yew behind it, although it overtops the hedge by a couple of yards. In a way, it provides its own firm architecture. We prune it every other year, shortening all its shoots back by two years' growth, which prevents it from becoming an uncontrolled tree. Furthermore, this treatment stimulates the growth of young shoots, which have a most attractive formality, inasmuch as the golden leaves are arranged along them in two ranks and overlap like feathers on a bird's wing or tiles on a roof. They provide a welcome variation of texture from the dense mass of the yew behind.

A happy conjuncture that happened unplanned, but at least I let it go on happening, was the seeding of a wand flower, *Dierama pulcherrimum*, against one of the topiary peacocks where they form a conversation piece (as shown in the photograph above). The double aster hedges lead up a sloping path to a pair of these peacocks and there, in front of them, is the wand flower, its pink bells arching over to the right and left and forward on the wire-tough but flexible stems that move constantly in the lightest breeze. Their contrast

tiles beneath its canopy. The entire roof had eventually to be retiled. Clematis montana and Wisteria sinensis have in the same way been equally destructive at Dixter in their time. I have learned that lesson at last, but I still rejoice to see the wonderful effect they create – provided, of course, that it occurs on someone else's roof.

Mainly for shape
Wall-trained fig trees were an original part of Dixter plantings. A large, well-indented leaf was required and this was provided by the variety 'Brunswick' (left). In favorable years, this also bears crops of the largest of any hardy fig.

Steps with extras
Lutyens's circular steps (opposite) lead down from the Long Border into the orchard, from which I have allowed oxeye daisies to stray and self-sow. They link this wholly informal meadow area to the steps' geometrical formality. On the platforms above the steps, one black mulberry survives from the original pair.

— • —

A transportation
Looking a little to the left of the opposite picture, you see the platform (below) once tenanted by the second mulberry. Behind is the entire elevation of a half-timbered house, dated about 1500, that once stood in a nearby village but was moved to Dixter when under threat of demolition.

with the solid topiary piece could not be more marked, hence the effect. I certainly would not claim that informal plants are always suited to architectural features. Much depends on the situation, and how they are used together. The loggia at the bottom of the Long Border, supported by Lutyens on tile pillars to replace its original, rotten walls, used to be covered by a huge mound, a veritable tree, of ivy – a dark and handsome lump, but utterly destructive of the

Ways with tulips

Tulips are my favorite spring bulbs (unless it's crocuses, depending on which happens to be blooming), and I grow a great many of them. This is largely because they like my heavy soil and increase on it, but that does not apply to species with small bulbs. Slugs devour them faster than they can grow, so I've ceased to struggle with most of these.

Some of my tulips have continued in the same spot as I originally planted them 25 years ago, without in any way diminishing. That means they have to be among plants that rarely or never need disturbing, or at the foot of shrubs that are still scrawny and threadbare in the spring; so I have the Parrot tulip 'Texas Gold' close to the summer-flowering *Tamarix pentandra* and to *Hydrangea* 'Mariesii', and they are also left undisturbed among the early-flowering day lily, *Hemerocallis lilioasphodelus*, which can be left pretty well indefinitely to its own devices.

Other tulips are treated as spring bedding plants, and these are lifted and stored for the summer. Mice are only too apt to eat them during this storage period so, after the bulbs are dried off on racks, we hang them up in net bags (such as those lemons or onions come in) on a pole stretched across two beams in an open-roofed shed.

At some time before planting, we sort through these bulbs, grading them by size into those that will flower in the next season and those that will certainly or perhaps not. The latter are lined out in a spare plot in the vegetable garden, to grow in size, which they do so effectively that our stocks keep on increasing. But then so does the number of places I keep thinking of in which to grow the tulips!

The early tulips

I do not at all fancy the big lumpy tulips that win prizes at flower shows but there is enough variety in flower shape and coloring to please everyone. We are pretty exposed to hostile spring winds, so I mainly concentrate on May flowerers, which are less likely to run into weather that batters them as soon as they open. Besides, I need decent weather to be able to enjoy the garden myself. If tulips can relax and open wide to the sun, that is when I, too, can relax.

Good companions
When I split and replant a group of hostas, I often interplant with tulips, as in the case of this Hosta *'Aureovariegata', whose yellow splashed leaves look good with the* Viridiflora *tulip 'Hollywood' (above).*

Flowering Parrots
Sometimes I leave my tulips where originally planted for 20 years or more; sometimes, as in the Long Border (left), they are treated as bedding, harvested after flowering, and replaced by some summer flowerer. 'Estella Rijnveld' (don't ask me how to pronounce her) is a jazzy Parrot tulip. The characteristically ragged petal margins give an informal air. The annual five-spot, Nemophilia maculata, *is growing in front and there is a single* Allium aflatunense, *overlooked when lifting others the previous year.*

Early and late
This early tulip, 'Couleur Cardinal' (right), was bedded with pomponette daisies, Bellis perennis, *sown late in the previous summer in a pot, pricked out, and then lined out to grow on. And they do, amazingly quickly. We finally planted up in late autumn. You never need to be in a great hurry with tulips, provided the bulbs are kept in a cool place. The yellow jonquil, 'Tittle Tattle', is a tail-ender of the narcissus season, usually at its best toward the end of spring. I leave the bulbs undisturbed, and their position is masked in summer by bedding plants.*

Still, I can't deny myself all the early kinds, and the first to open, of which I have a plentiful supply, is the Fosteriana hybrid, 'Purissima' (syn. 'White Emperor'). It has a large, long bloom (ivory at first, maturing to pure white) on a short-ish stem, above broad, glaucous leaves. I usually bed it among F1 'Crescendo Red' polyanthus, which I initially raised from seed and have since increased by division. They flower early and an early tulip is needed to coincide with this. Polyanthus develop a sickness if grown too often in the same soil, so I have to move this bedding combination around.

My main bedding-out area is in front of the house. It varies in content from year to year, but tulips are rarely excluded. One spring, above a carpet of red pomponette daisies, *Bellis perennis*, I had the late red tulip, 'Halcro', which has a nice

Watch it, Lloyd
This year I did the main bedding-out area in front of the house with the late red tulip 'Halcro', the Lily-flowered tulip 'China Pink' and red pomponette daisies (top). My niece described the result as "dire." She may have been right, but so what?

Nonstop show
I have kept my F1 'Crescendo Red' polyanthus plants (originally from seed) for several years now. As they flower early, I grow them with the early Fosteriana tulip, 'Purissima' (above), which expands to a large, beautifully shaped chalice.

In trouble again

This time it's pink and yellow (left). But why not? I should like to do a pink and yellow border. The wallflowers are 'Purple Queen' and the wonderfully vital yellow 'Cloth of Gold'. As the latter is so much the more assertive, I used two plants of purple to every one of yellow. I think tulips look better in blocks behind, in front of, or among wallflowers than scattered between them. The tulips are the Lily-flowered 'China Pink' and mauve and white 'Magier', which is classified as Single Late (which includes the Darwins). To get decent plants, you must grow your own wallflowers from seed.

The sweet disease

This Rembrandt tulip (below), once of uniform coloring, has now become "broken" as a result of infection by viruses. All the Rembrandt tulips were infected in this way, but the European Community does not now allow the deliberate marketing of infected bulbs. You just have to wait for it to happen in your own garden, which it soon does. The vigor of the bulb is reduced, but not seriously.

Fond of Parrots
In all tulips, the background color is either white or yellow, but this only shows up when the overlying color becomes broken. That is often the case with Parrot tulips. 'Flaming Parrot' (above) has a yellow ground.

In the green
Viridiflora tulips are banded with green along the centers of the outer segments. Here is 'Spring Green' (right), planted among Hosta *'Krossa Regal'.* Epimedium pinnatum *'Colchicum' is in the foreground.*

elongated bloom, and the Lily-flowered 'China Pink'. The main reason for combining these two colors, admittedly not to everyone's taste, was that I had enough bulbs of the two, and only of these two, to fill a large area. They weren't too bad! Next year, behind a mix in the ratio of two to one of 'Purple Queen' and 'Cloth of Gold' wallflowers (fewer plants are needed of the stronger color), tulips were grouped in colors that would not quarrel with these two.

— **Parrots and Lilies** —

Among my favorite tulip shapes are the Parrot and Lily-flowered classes. Parrots typically have informally curving stems and ragged-edged blooms streaked with green along the center of the outer petals, at least while the flower is young. 'Orange Favorite' I grow among late perennials like *Rudbeckia sullivantii* 'Goldsturm' in the Long Border. There is a subtle pink flush in its orange coloring. 'Texas Gold', at the top of the border, is almost the latest of all to flower. 'Flaming Parrot', in crimson and yellow, works well and is not so disturbing as 'Estella Rijnveld', a startling contrast in red and white but totally acceptable in the Long Border with forget-me-nots, the mauve globes of *Allium aflatunense* and the

greens of much spring foliage. You merely need to stand back a little. Perhaps half close your eyes.

Among the Lily-flowereds, 'White Triumphator', tall and graceful, is arguably the finest white tulip of all. You'll like it against a shaded background, interplanted with yellow doronicums (of which I lost all my stock, and serves me right, when treating the ground with simazine). The two yellows that I fancy are 'Golden Duchess', with broader petals, and 'West Point', in which the segments are narrow and pointed. I have interplanted the magenta-flowered *Bergenia* 'Ballawley Hybrid' with these. Such startling contrasts are welcome in spring, when so much is green, but the bergenia has not yet played its part too well. I live in hope. I have also contrasted it with the scarlet Lily-flowered tulip, 'Dyanito', and was pleased when this aroused comment.

Among lupines, I recently grew the Lily-flowered tulip 'Marilyn', which is white, feathered with purplish red, and the purple Lily-flowered 'Burgundy'. 'Greuze', which is a more traditional cup shape, is of the same somber coloring as 'Burgundy', and it really does need to be highlighted, as it might be in a planting of 'Primrose Monarch' wallflowers with their attractive pale yellow flowers.

Viridiflora tulips, with a large dose of green in each flower, can be fun. When replanting some hostas, I included 'Spring Green', which has a Lily-flowered shape and is in very pale and darker green; I also included 'Hollywood', an extraordinary combination of metallic green and oxblood red. Unfortunately, a proportion of the blooms are deformed and, as a result, they then never open properly.

Good partners

Ways to use tulips are fascinating to think up. I hope I have a good one coming along with the tall red 'Halcro' rising from amid a lacy network of giant fennel, *Ferula communis*, foliage. There are four widely spaced plants of the latter in the Wall Garden. They rise to 8ft (2.3m) on flowering in June, then die away quickly, so that there is time to interplant with yet another bedding or annual ingredient for the season's tail end. Multiflowered tulips, in which there are one, two, or three blooms to a stem, are excellent in a garden setting, as the flowers are numerous without ever, even on first being purchased, looking over-large or coarse. 'Georgette' is the one I have grown in some quantity. At first pale yellow, even a little anemic, the color deepens, then develops orange streaks, and finishes entirely orange. Quite a metamorphosis. When I planted it among later flowering sweet williams, it looked good with a snowy white background of the shrub *Exochorda* x *macrantha* 'The Bride'.

The season's end

Grown with sweet williams, tulips can be harvested fully ripened in July, prior to following the sweet williams with late-sown annuals. (More about this on pages 102-5.) If combined with a May-flowering bedding plant, however, they'll be lifted green and are better not replanted in a trench but laid out on racks in a cool, dry place, where the nourishment in the foliage will be returned to the bulbs. When they are dry, you can sort them out and bag the bulbs for the summer. They can then be replanted in their new surroundings in the early months of autumn.

The last of all my tulips to flower is the species *Tulipa sprengeri*, at the turn of May-June. About 2ft (60cm) tall, it has pointed blooms that are brick-red inside, buff without. This is expensive to buy, but it makes lots of seed, and, if grown where the ground is left more or less undisturbed, it will usually self-sow and colonize well.

LIFTING
Tulips

Many gardeners need to replace their tulips at frequent intervals, but if your soil is on the stiff side, the tulips will often, under border conditions, maintain their populations. If treated as spring bedding, to be followed by summer annuals or bedders, tulips must often be lifted while still green. Do not replant them, but dry them off on racks in an airy shed.

When the tops are quite sere, detach them from the bulbs and grade these into ones that look large enough to flower next year and ones that do not. If you have the space in your garden, the latter can be lined out, in autumn, to grow on. In this way, you will soon build up your tulip stocks materially.

Latest of all
The Parrot tulip 'Texas Gold' (above) never flowers before the middle of May. As the bloom ages, it becomes margined and streaked with red. My clumps at the top of the Long Border have been established for at least 25 years, in positions where they never need to be disturbed – for instance, among day lilies, the suckering Hemerocallis flava *(now known as* H. lilioasphodelus*).*

Foliage plants

FLOWERS MAY make the headlines (or book titles) and draw the crowds more than foliage, but the substance of a garden is in its leaves. Flowers are the icing on the cake. If a good foliage plant also bears worthwhile flowers, that is a great bonus, but the limitations of flowers unsupported by good leaves soon become apparent.

I have written a whole book on foliage plants and they are emphasized in many chapters here – on bamboos, ferns, and grasses, for a start. Others remain, waiting to be drawn into our magic circle. Gray foliage plants, for instance. In our climate, I find that these grays look their best on a sunny day in autumn, following a heavy overnight dew, which has left them more silver than gray. The lusher kinds, which are rather tender, also reach their climax at the end of a long summer's growing season. Once the frosts become marked, the situation changes rapidly. Gray foliage under dull winter skies looks miserable, which was why Graham Stuart Thomas left it out of his book, *Colour in the Winter Garden*.

—— *Gray-leaved plants* ——

I don't grow gray foliage in any great quantity. Our heavy clay soil doesn't bring out the best in it. I love *Centaurea gymnocarpa* and have an excellent form of it, which I keep going from cuttings. Never try to grow seedlings. They aren't nearly pale

Winter shapes

Many of the evergreen Australian gum trees, like Eucalyptus gunnii *(right), have rounded juvenile foliage, though in maturity the leaves become lance shaped. Hard annual pruning retains the juvenile leaf type. Several evergreen spurges resemble* Euphorbia x martinii, *also seen here behind the eucalyptus.*

enough and they flower too much. That spoils them. The leaves are long in a double comb, but each comb tooth itself has projections. The total effect is lacy but there is still a design to it. *Senecio vira-vira* (syn. *S. leucostachys*) has less design; its double combs are shorter. But, with a rambling habit, it is a wonderful filler. Mine looked good next to 'The Fairy', a pink Polyanthus rose. *Helichrysum petiolare*, with its felted gray heart-shaped leaves, has a most adaptable habit. I use it in my ornamental pots for the summer, and it soon conceals their rims with its wide-spreading habit.

Its lime-green-leaved variant, 'Limelight', has rather different requirements, because it scorches in sun, especially if dry at the root. Another trait worth remarking on is that its leaves glisten and are at their brightest when wet after rain, whereas the grays are then all spotty and at their least presentable. 'Limelight' combines well in a container, or in neighboring containers, with the tuberous-rooted *Begonia sutherlandii*, which has a mass of tiny pale orange flowers.

A quite different helichrysum is *Helichrysum splendidum*, a stiffly growing hardy shrub. All its young shoots grow bolt upright, the cluster of terminal leaves forming tight rosettes. This becomes a hopelessly sprawling shrub if not regularly and hard pruned in early spring. It then makes dense hummocks, some 18in (45cm) tall, good at a border's margin. Its clusters of small yellow flowers are a letdown and undesirable, but there'll be none if you prune as I suggest. I have it in front of a couple of soft-textured conifers, *Chamaecyparis thyoides* 'Ericoides', which makes a seagreen cone of juvenile foliage,

Calm resting point

The main emphasis midway along my Long Border of mixed planting is on foliage (left). We prune Dickson's golden elm, at the back, all over every other year. We do this partly to prevent it becoming an uncontrollably large tree and partly to promote plenty of young shoots, along which the leaves lie in two ranks. The willows, in front, are Salix alba 'Sericea'.

Damp border

Hosta leaves contrast well in shape and texture with those of rodgersias (right). Hosta 'Buckshaw Blue' *is at its best from May to June. It is the favorite food of slugs and snails, in contrast to* Rodgersia pinnata, *whose leathery leaves they do not touch. This is a pink-flowered form that was given to me unnamed. Right at the back you can see the foliage of* Aralia cachemirica.

turning purple in winter. The two, the helichrysum and the chamaecyparis, are excellent foils one to the other.

Of the artemisias, my favorite is *Artemisia arborescens*, if only it were hardier. It has a loose, open habit and should grow fast, making an impression in its first year from a cutting. Occasionally it survives for a second. Sparrows picking off the leaves for their nests often ruin my plants. I like it among the white Japanese anemones. It also looks good with the panicles of red, tubular *Phygelius capensis* growing through.

The arrival of *Artemisia* 'Powis Castle' on the scene a few decades ago was a great event. Hardy (almost), nonflowering, and more compact than *A. arborescens*, but never stodgy, it softens bright flowers like pink *Nerine* x *bowdenii* and *Aster novae-angliae* 'Alma Pötschke'. (It is a martyr to black aphids and you should always be on the lookout.) Pink and gray go so well together. Thus, *Artemisia ludoviciana* 'Silver Queen' surrounding a bush or two of *Hebe* 'Great Orme' looks very good.

— *Unusual features* —

If gray foliage is enhanced by heavy late-summer and autumn dews, so are other hairy leaves, notably *Bergenia ciliata*, of which you should avoid the variety *ligulata*, because its leaves are not so big, nor are they nearly so deeply felted with fur. This bergenia is deciduous, and it thus avoids the fault in many of its genus of being disagreeably leathery. Its leaves are soft and, in a moist, shady situation, they grow very large. I combine it with the contrasting leaves of the Bamboo, *Arundinaria falconeri* (described in the Bamboo chapter, see pages 148-51), a finely dissected male fern, *Dryopteris filix-mas* 'Linearis', and the palmate leaves of *Rodgersia podophylla*.

The inflorescences, rather than the leaves, of *Cotinus coggygria* (also known as the smoke bush) are great dew catchers and I grow the green-leaved type plant for that. But I also grow the slightly greenish purple 'Foliis Purpureis', now designated 'Rubrifolius' (none too appropriately), which I have in two places. In the Long Border it teams up with the purple globes of *Allium christophii* and another good companion, here, is a sedge, *Carex muskinguemensis*, with bright green linear leaves arranged in threes along an 18in (45cm) stem. My second cotinus is in lieu of a yew on the topiary lawn, as these shrubs make excellent specimens. In some years, its foliage takes on thrilling autumn color, with translucent incandescence.

Always lively
Libertia peregrinans *(left) is an evergreen perennial from New Zealand, with 12in (30cm) tall leaves of a bronzy coloring. They never look dull but are at their brightest and most noticeable in winter. White flowers are followed by persistent fruits.*

Never mind the path
Up to a point, and if you don't mind being unable to walk two abreast, it looks comfortable to see plants splurging over path (or lawn) margins. The foreground grass (right) is Stipa arundinacea. *Two bush ivies (left) are backed by the golden form of* Catalpa bignonioides, *which I keep as a bush by hard pruning.*

Important parents
The numerous, closely set leaflets belong to Mahonia lomariifolia, *a rather tender species flowering in early winter (above). The other is* M. japonica, *whose lily-of-the-valley-scented flowers open between November and March. These two species have been crossed, the hybrids being classified as* M. x media.

My third cotinus, 'Royal Purple', does not smoke. I grow it in the Long Border entirely for its rich purple foliage, where it is a focus for the many good flowers described in the High Summer chapter on pages 70-79.

Fuchsia magellanica 'Versicolor', perfectly hardy with me, like many fuchsias generally gives of its best in September-October. I cut it right down in winter and the young shoot tips sprout in exciting shades of pink when they start growing, but it goes into the doldrums in summer, with ashen foliage and few flowers. Then, in autumn, it takes on a new lease, sprouts with colorful young foliage again and flowers abundantly, its

3ft- (90cm-) long, pliable branches bowing down under the weight of quantities of blossom.

As you would expect, much foliage is brightest and cleanest in spring. *Valeriana phu* 'Aurea' is a hardy perennial that retains its basal leaves through the winter, when they are a quite ordinary green. In March they change to a quite extraordinary lime-green. To make use of this transformation, I have planted the early *Scilla bifolia* around the valerian. This has racemes of rich blue flowers.

Ribes alpinum 'Aureum', growing among the stems of a 'Frühlingsgold' rose, breaks into leaf of lime-green coloring,

not long afterward. It is a pretty, twiggy bush, quite slow growing, and no more than 3ft (90cm) tall after many years.

Anything with a yellow leaf is apt to scorch in the hot sunshine of early summer. So it is with the mock orange, *Philadelphus coronarius* 'Aureus'. It is ravishingly fresh in spring. If you treat it entirely as a foliage plant, pruning it hard back in winter, it seldom scorches on the resulting young growth. But if you leave these shoots to carry their heavy-scented blossom the next year, they'll scorch with the slightest excuse. The green-and-white-leaved *P. coronarius* 'Variegatus' is rather liable to scorch, too, but it is so pretty when the new foliage

Important corner

Making a loud noise at the corner where a path crosses the Long Border (left) is the explosive-looking Yucca gloriosa 'Variegata'. When it flowers, this rosette will die and be replaced by a pair of smaller ones. I would prefer it not to flower. The grass behind, Miscanthus sinensis 'Silver Feather', will flower elegantly in early autumn, by which time its legs look rather bare, so I have planted the Long Border's only conifer, Pinus mugo, in front to do a covering act. The blue flower, which also has metallic blue stems, is Eryngium × oliverianum. Its thick, fleshy roots hate disturbance and have received none for at least 50 years.

Smoke bush

This, the green-leaved Cotinus coggygria (left), is hardly a foliage plant, though its flaming autumn tints can be spectacular in a good year. The "smoke" of its inflorescences, pink in sunlight, green in shade, and, finally, gray (wig bush is another name), is the main attraction. It makes a good lawn specimen. The deep purple-leaved forms are grown entirely for their foliage.

combines with the white flowers that I would not recommend hard pruning for that. I have it planted in a bit of shade, which seems to protect it a little.

Most variegated plants give no scorch trouble. *Weigela florida* 'Variegata' is probably the oldest shrub in the Long Border. It carries swags of pale pink funnels in May, when its young leaves are green with a white margin, and then continues to pay its rent right through to late autumn, the foliage having matured to a yellow variegation. I have a green and white variegated sweet chestnut, *Castanea sativa* 'Albovariegata', quite near to this, and it has grown so well that it has become embarrassingly large, so I have recently lopped it.

Another foliage tree on the Long Border, which I have had for 40 years but needed to shorten back once in its lifetime (to date), is an unarmed clone called 'Elegantissima' of the thorny honey locust, *Gleditsia triacanthos*. It forms a tall cone on a prominent corner where an ancient apple grew until about 1950 (when it died of honey fungus). The first example I saw of this was on the grounds of the famous old nursery of Jackman, in Woking, Surrey. It was January, but the tree had a presence, as slow growers so often do. In winter, you can see the nest used by a wood pigeon in summer. She makes little crooning noises under her breath while I'm on my knees weeding beneath. It is not until late in May that this tree flushes, with pinnate green leaves that remain fresh till shed.

— *Changing leaf color* —

Much foliage becomes wan in its color or variegation, when grown in shade. The variety of common elder, *Sambucus nigra*, called 'Marginata', does not fade. The marginal variegation of its leaves, pale yellow when young, maturing white, will show up well at a distance in the thickened gloom of an evergreen, overhanging tree (postulating the toughest assignation I can think of). Now, with the golden cut-leaved elder, *S. racemosa* 'Plumosa Aurea', it is different. In deep shade, that

becomes a pasty yellow. But some shade and plenty of moisture are appreciated, because it is liable to scorch in hot, dry conditions. Another way in which the leaf display can be spoiled is by letting the shrub flower. The foliage will be smaller and more prone to scorching. The flowers are nothing, anyway. So I prune my pair hard, every winter, and that entirely eliminates flowering. At first the young foliage is copper, then changing through deep, ocherous yellow to a lighter, more green-tinted shade. The leaves are lacily toothed at their margins. Where I grow mine is described in the High Summer chapter on pages 80-89.

A similar progress in changing leaf color occurs in a very different shrub, the popular *Spiraea japonica* 'Goldflame'. A height of 3ft (90cm) is ideal for this spiraea, if properly pruned, and it should be constantly renewed by the entire removal of old branches every year. I do this immediately after its early-summer flowering. The flowers are pink and cause the more sensitive of my fellow mortals to shudder. I think they look all right in a lime-green setting but not once have they turned brown, on dying. That's when I set to and sort them out. This in turn, means that I have no pruning to do in early spring (the normally recommended season), but can immediately enjoy the early flush of new foliage. I have planted some pink hyacinths in front of my bush and like their contribution a lot.

Fresh in winter

The plant we have known as Arum italicum 'Pictum', but some botanists would now have us call A. italicum italicum (right), is a winter favorite both with flower arrangers (I love to pick snowdrops with it) and with gardeners. New foliage appears from October.

— *Big is beautiful* —

I must try and convey the excitement of the giant fennel, *Ferula communis*, which only makes its appearance as an extra in the tulip chapter on page 33. Forget about food and fish; it is only distantly related to the herb, *Foeniculum vulgare*, and itself has no aroma. Next to the gunnera, its leaves are the largest in my garden, but they are dissected into such a fine filigree network that any sense of volume is entirely dissipated. Putting in their first tentative appearance in January, they (perhaps only three to a plant) steadily expand through the next five months until, at a height of about 4ft (1.2m), they have built a fresh green, undulating platform of the greatest delicacy. It is a plant that deserves a lot of space, so that you can plant, say, half a dozen together in one colony, spacing them 4ft (1.2m) apart. *F. communis* doesn't flower every year

and the leaves are the main thing, but when it does flower, the excitement becomes almost unbearable. A thick, fleshy shoot suddenly appears and within three weeks it is a branching inflorescence 8ft (2.3m) high, opening into pierced platforms of greeny yellow flowers. But there has to be an anticlimax. Within another three weeks, the entire plant has died away except for the now blackening inflorescence.

The voluptuous energy of a big herbaceous plant, which disappears from sight for half the year but then returns with breathtaking panache, is found also in the herbaceous aralias. The one I grow is *Aralia cachemirica*. I have to admit that it has not done as well as I should like in the past two or three years. I fancy it has lacked the moisture it requires when in full growth. But when the American landscape architect, Wolfgang Oehme, saw it laden with fruit a few years ago, he was so impressed that half the crop went home with him. It propagates easily from seed and the plant is totally hardy, so I hope he has done well with it. It unfolds large pinnate leaves on stems which, when suited, may grow 7ft (2.1m) or more high and terminate in a panicle of small, globular umbels (like an ivy's, to which it is related). These are nothing much, but they ripen into crops of purple-black berries, subtended by purple stalks and stems. You then appreciate what style the beast has.

— *Plants with waxy leaves* —

I have to work up to my favorite of all the foliage plants in this garden through others with glaucous, which is to say waxy, blue leaves. If raindrops are held on them they coalesce into large, light-reflecting globules, ready like quicksilver to take flight if disturbed by the slightest movement. Some of the spurges belong here; *Euphorbia myrsinites*, *E. nicaeensis* and my favorite *E. rigida* which, however, is not as hardy as the rest,

A popular spiraea
Spiraea japonica 'Goldflame' (above) was earliest on the scene of a comparatively recent range within this species, grown principally for their colorful foliage. It starts coppery, in early spring, maturing to yellowy green in early summer. By that time it will be carrying its flattened heads of pink flowers. When these turn brown, I give the shrub its annual pruning, removing all the older branches entirely, and shortening the strong young ones enough to cut out the faded blossom. As new foliage will be made during the summer months, spring pruning will not therefore be necessary.

MAINTAINING
Melianthus

I consider that *Melianthus major* has the most beautiful foliage of any plant we can treat as hardy, or nearly so. I have had my colony for more than 20 years, but hardiness depends on getting a planting well established before it encounters a vicious winter. And, during that season, I pack sere fern fronds between its stems as a protection for its roots. In our climate, it is generally killed to the ground in winter, and then starts again from below soil level in spring. If top growth does survive, I cut it right back anyway, in spring, because this produces a nice, compact mass of foliage. In mild areas, where old growth is preserved, it becomes a gangling and untidy shrub. The flowers, and the interest, soon evaporate.

Contrast in form and texture
This spring foliage background to grape hyacinths (right) is made by the extremely delicate young fronds of a hardy maidenhair fern, Adiantum pedatum, *and the tough, shiny, strap leaves of colchicums. The fern is a good-tempered clump-former and would really prefer a bit of overhead shade in hot weather, but I tired of the shrub that was producing this. The rhododendron that has replaced it is slow growing and not yet up to its shade-producing job.*

Flowers and foliage
A winter photograph, when Sarcococca hookeriana digyma *(above) carries tiny, heavily scented blossom. Sprigs of male and female* Skimmia japonica *show the latter in fruit, and the former, in the clone 'Rubella', with a reddish flush on flower buds and leaf margins.*

and I am wondering where to try it next. Its columns of sharply pointed lance leaves (on a fairly low plant) have a sculptural quality best appreciated in low winter sunshine, when each leaf casts shadows on its neighbors.

The shrubby *Kniphofia caulescens* is a noble plant, ever-green, though looking its worst in winter. It makes pineapple-like rosettes of glaucous foliage and can build into a handsome colony that is best seen in a rocky surround (no rocks at Dixter) or in an expanse of gravel (no gravel, either). Leeks are the plants it most closely resembles. If you divide and replant it frequently, it will be generous, in September, with its fairly short-stemmed spikes of coral pokers.

And so we come to *Melianthus major* (as anyone familiar with my writings will have guessed). I make no apology for its

being considered a weed in warmer climates. That's their lookout. It can also become a scrawny shrub if it brings its old growth through the winter and is not pruned back to the ground in spring, which it should always be for best foliage effect. And that, after all, is the whole point. The leaves are large, pinnate, deeply toothed along their margins, and very glaucous. Like *Euphorbia rigida*, they create steely, three-dimensional sculptures in low sunlight, autumn being the plant's best season, but the leaves generally remain in excellent condition through to December.

In our climate, it is then wise to cover the roots with protective fern fronds. I have never lost a plant in 40 years, but a question mark will hang over it until it is truly settled in. It is beautiful with Japanese anemones in white or in pink.

The meadows

WE HAVE at least half a dozen areas of rough grass within the garden, some of them quite centrally located, which occasions surprise, even disgust, in visitors from a conventional background. I admit that just before their first annual cut in late summer, they can look like overblown hay patches.

But permanent and long-established meadows, if not allowed to be invaded by self-sowing scrub, do harbor a most beautiful assortment of herbs, whether bulbs, grasses or colorful perennials. Most plant lovers have experienced the breathtaking richness and variety in a Swiss alpine meadow before it is cut for hay, and I think it can be said that the climate of Europe does generally suit this medium, and that a great range of flowers can take advantage of it.

At any rate, it certainly appealed to my mother, who first fostered the meadow idiom within the more formal architectural elements at Dixter. So when you enter the modest front gate and follow the straight flagstone path towards our porch, the yew-hedge-enclosed area to right and to left was rough grass from the first. It is so packed with good plants that, in planting even more, you almost inevitably disturb or chop in half others that came before. Not all the work has to be done

Moon daisies

At the turn of May and June, the orchard is alive with moon, or ox-eye, daisies (left). Their populations vary greatly over the years, and I believe that moisture is the principal factor affecting them. Excellent displays appear at the same time as yellow hawkbits (Leontodon), but these are not fully open until around 11 o'clock in the morning.

———•———

Native and introduced

Red clover (below) flowers in abundance at the same time as the moon daisies and hawkbits, but at a lower level. Clovers are often left out of meadow-seed mixtures for domestic use, probably because they enrich the soil by nitrogen fixation, whereas a poor soil enables the richest flora to co-exist. Camassia quamash, a North American native, was my introduction at a time when its bulbs were cheap. They no longer are.

Front meadow
These are the flowering lawns (above) that you first encounter on entering the front gate. Most of the color at the turn of March and April is provided by our native daffodil, Narcissus pseudo-narcissus, *which my mother raised from seed.*

May scene
May is the season of Camassia quamash (top), *a bulb eaten by the North American Indians in its native habitats. It spreads both by clumping up and self-sowing. The seeds ripen in July and I await this signal before grass cutting starts.*

by the gardener. His task is to give the tapestry contents a good start and then merely make it congenial for them to increase with the minimum of further interference.

Remember that most grassland plants like full exposure to sunlight and poor soil. The poorer the soil, the more varied its contents. Once you start to enrich it, for instance by leaving grass mowings to rot *in situ*, certain greedy plants, like cow parsley, will benefit at the expense of others, which will be elbowed out. There are two floral seasons. The first runs from January to July. As it starts with quite tiny snowdrops and crocuses, the turf needs to be mown as tight as possible, almost as close as a lawn. If the ground remains firm, we mow over it even as late as early December. Later than that, you run into trouble with the bulbs' young snouts.

There are exceptions to the full exposure precept. Snowdrops clump up more happily where the turf is a bit thin, as on the north side of the front path yew hedge where there is also shade from the wild pear tree. The 90 or so bulbs that I planted here in the 1950s have increased prodigiously. Quite exciting to be the instrument, really, though I have always been notably unsuccessful in pleasing winter aconites.

Thorny specimen
Moon daisies and hawkbits are joined, along the front path, by the June flowering of a hawthorn, Crataegus laciniata (left). This was a replacement for one of the five walnuts originally planted in this area. The thorn makes an excellent small specimen tree, with crops of spectacular orange haws in October.

Native ingredients
Shown (above) with the fine leaves of the vetch Vicia cracca, which has masses of blue flowers in dense spikes just before the grass is cut.

Snowdrops are at their peak in February and so are the winter crocuses. They love our heavy soil and are little troubled by mice or voles, which like to make their runs in lighter ground. So we first have *Crocus chrysanthus* 'Snow Bunting', which is deliciously scented, if you can be bothered to get down to sniff it. Other forms of this species cover the entire range of crocus colors and, because they constantly interbreed, you'll find that you're not just growing the named varieties that you originally planted.

Crocus tommasinianus is one of the earliest and a great self-seeder. Its wan, toothpick buds open in sunshine to mauve stars and contrast cheerfully with the rich orange of *C. flavus*. From this last, the common yellow Dutch hybrid derives.

That, too, is early; it clumps up well but is sterile, not setting seed, so if you want to increase its range you should lift a few clumps as soon as they have flowered, split them into individual corms and replant over a wider area.

In the way they open wide to sunshine, crocuses really proclaim to the world when there's sun and warmth to be enjoyed. They are among the most gladdening of flowers and are heavily attended by bees, foraging for pollen to feed their young brood. The Dutch hybrids of *Crocus vernus*, mainly in shades of white, mauve, and purple, many of them stripy, are at their peak in March. Because they seed so freely, they make extensive carpets rather than clumps. These are concentrated in our old orchard and upper moat, which my parents had drained on coming to Dixter. It is shaped like a bath. Having been turf only since 1912 or so, the grasses here, even now, tend to grow faster and more rankly than in the really old turf, so they need more frequent cutting: three times a year.

Flower tapestry

The upper moat was where my mother first concentrated her efforts to make the Botticelli Garden (having his *Primavera* in mind). She planted here all the spare polyanthus, originally used for spring bedding, and these old strains still hold their own against all comers. Then she raised the British native snakeshead fritillary, *Fritillaria meleagris*, from seed, over many years, eventually planting the seedlings directly from the boxes into which they were pricked out onto the moat banks and, later, into the orchard and by the front path. They were the typical purple and the albino forms and, when self-sowing took over, as it soon did in the heavy ground that they love, many intermediate colors grew.

My mother was apt to plant on the moat banks, rather than at the bottom, where she thought it would be too wet, but the plants thought otherwise. Fritillaries, crocuses, and *Anemone apennina* have spread down here, and I have added a purple form of "English" iris, *Iris latifolia* (not English at all, actually), which is perfectly comfortable there. My father saw to it that the moat had a thoroughly efficient drain. There is a big patch of snowflakes, *Leucojum aestivum*, flowering in March-April, and the terrace wall behind, covered with mauve aubrieta, provides a cheerful background.

Meanwhile the orchard, which is just alongside, follows the crocuses with a display of traditional daffodils and narcissi, with varieties that were fashionable in the early years of the century. They were planted in alternating drifts of yellow and

Early crocuses
In the front meadows I have a great concentration of the different forms of Crocus chrysanthus *(left). Smaller and earlier flowering than the Dutch hybrids, this is a variable species. If you buy named varieties and plant them side by side, they'll hybridize, with interesting results.*

Wild tapestry
Primroses, wood anemones, wild daffodils and snakeshead fritillaries (below) are all growing together like the background to the medieval unicorn tapestries.

Another happy orchid
Biggest and boldest of the native orchids that colonize the meadows at Dixter (especially the upper moat), are the early purples, Orchis mascula *(far left), already at their showiest in mid-spring.*

Pop-up plant
The dog's tooth violet, Erythronium dens-canis *(left), appears suddenly in mid-March, and is in bloom within two or three days. Its foliage is handsomely marbled. To increase it, clumps are best split after flowering.*

The first meadow

The area where my mother first started her meadow gardening was on the site of the drained upper moat (above). Celandines come of their own accord and open wide to the sun. The polyanthus, once bedded out for the spring, she transferred here after they had flowered, and they have survived all those years.

Late on the scene

By May, the orchard's display of daffodils has all faded, apart from the pheasant's eyes, Narcissus poeticus 'Recurvus' (left). These are most deliciously scented, which makes them especially good to pick. There is a loosely double form of them that flowers even later.

white, not, on the whole, mixing the varieties. This is sound practice. Mixtures tend to confuse the eye. These daffodils also cover different seasons. 'Princeps', which is really just a tetraploid and large form of the British native trumpet daffodil, *Narcissus pseudonarcissus* (the Lent lily), is first out, in late March, while the poet's narcissus, with its delicious scent, makes its contribution in May. This is *N. poeticus recurvus* and derives from the wilding seen in Swiss and French meadows.

My mother grew a great many Lent lilies from seed, but these were mainly planted on the front meadow, where small things are appropriate to the scale.

— The orchids —

One good feature about the orchard, for which I am grateful, is that the daffodil areas are not too pervasive. Each group has a wide margin of green sward dividing it from the next. These clearer areas allow space for the dominance of wild features like the green-winged orchids, *Orchis morio*, that are such a delight throughout May, not to mention more ordinary but abundant things like moon daisies, yellow hawkbits and red clover. Thus dying daffodil foliage, which is such a worry to many gardeners, becomes scarcely noticed here, as other plants take over and absorb it.

Two other locally wild orchids are abundant in our meadows. The early purples, *Orchis mascula*, with heavily blotched foliage and often quite substantial spikes of rosy purple flowers in April, make their biggest impression in the upper moat, but they also have self-sown in many other places. The spotted orchids, *Dactylorhiza fuchsii*, are even more ardent self-sowers and appear in undisturbed places, like paving cracks, all over the garden. Their spikes are mauve and these are at their best in June.

— At the start of summer —

I must not leave out a striking May feature in the front path meadow: the blue stars, born in short spikes, of the North American *Camassia quamash*. In a predominantly green, yellow, and white setting, blue stands out fantastically. For some years after the Second World War, bulbs were very cheap to buy and I would purchase a hundred every autumn. They have clumped and self-sown, and flower most freely when the summer of the previous year was hot. Their seeds do not ripen

Daffodil orchard

The orchard (above) was planted around 1912 with daffodil varieties that were fashionable then. None, in those days, was as coarse and muscular as the breeders have made them since, so they fit well into a landscape setting. They were arranged in groups of the same variety, which is always more effective than mixtures, which confuse the eye: yellow alternating with white, and the early 'Princeps' divorced from the mid-season varieties. Plenty of green breathing space was left between plantings, and crocuses are a lively feature a month earlier.

STARTING A
Meadow

The most stable meadows, and those that have the richest tapestry of flowers, are those made in old turf as they are at Dixter. If you got tired of mowing a long-established and none-too-well cared for lawn, and simply let it grow, that would be an ideal start to a meadow. The plants you wanted to introduce would then be best sown in pots or in short rows in the garden; lined out at a suitable spacing; then, when strong enough, transferred to the meadow after the grass had been cut (for it must be cut at least once a year) in the autumn when the ground was soft again.

until well into July, so it is important not to cut the grass until the last week of that month.

At the end of June there are still many meadow flowers to enjoy. The blue meadow cranesbill was one of my mother's favorites, and it has a number of strongholds where she originally planted it, and where it self-sowed subsequently. One of these is close to the Horse Pond with another alongside the back drive, where I have added in the white-flowered form. Here, also, the tufted vetch, *Vicia cracca*, makes swathes of blue in July, some of them garlanding the yew hedges. The earlier-mentioned 'English' irises also flower at the turn of June-July, while the common bent, a fine-leaved grass, flowers as late as this, creating a pink haze that is particularly enchanting when laden with dew on a summer's morning. So our late grass-cutting practices do not irk me at all.

— *Trees in the meadow* —

The cuts made between now and December all help to reduce turf vigor and coarseness; for the same reason, we make them as close as possible. The first of them in late summer bites into brown old grass stems, and the orchard looks the color of a desert, no matter whether the ground is moist or dry. You can then appreciate, from its undulations, that this was once plowed land, done in the medieval way, which threw it up into wide ridges and furrows. The ridges were later planted with fruit trees, when this became an orchard, and that was well before our time. Because so many birds attack fruit, and

because the starvation conditions that favor a rich flora do not favor fruit (apples tend to have the consistency of wood), I have, for years, been planting small trees of any kind I fancy. My mother derisively observed that I was turning it into a botanic garden, and she had a point. But, with all our predominating yew hedges, there are not many areas suitable for trees at Dixter and yet there are many with which I want a close acquaintance. In this way I defend my practice, but I have to admit that the conditions do not suit a proportion of my trees at all well.

Once the grass has greened up again, following this first cut, it becomes studded with yellow daisies, so even August is not a dull month in this department, for those with eyes to see. At the end of that month, the colchicums begin the meadows' second season, which lasts until the end of October, and is contributed to mainly by them and by the real autumn crocuses. I have principally planted these in the front meadow, and the cheapest way to obtain material for this purpose is by growing them in various pieces of cultivated borders, for

Water meadow native
The snakeshead fritillary, Fritillaria meleagris *(right), loves damp, heavy soil, whether clay or alluvial, but not waterlogged. Bulbs are not expensive to buy and, given a good start, they will self-sow, but this takes time and can't be hurried.*

A small cheat
This narcissus (left) is not actually growing in meadow turf but it could have been, as most kinds of daffodil colonize easily in grassland if it is not too dry. The coarser, heavier types leave the worst legacy of dying foliage.

———— • ————

From formal to informal
The wall of the lower terrace (right) is colonized by red valerian, Centranthus ruber, *and its white-flowered albino form. Then, beneath a strip of mown grass, the upper moat, now meadow, begins.*

a start. There they will increase rapidly and the thinned-out colonies can then be transferred to the rough grass. We have a wonderfully efficient bulb-planting tool, dating back 80 years. It seems crazy that it has gone out of commerce. If you have planting to do in August-September, the ground tends to be iron-hard and it needs to be irrigated for the best part of 24 hours before the bulb planter can be used.

Colchicums and crocuses

Colchicums are either white *Colchicum autumnale* 'Album' and *C. speciosum* 'Album' – or in some pinkish shade of lilac or mauve. The crocuses, though similarly shaped, never have that pinkish color. The two that thrive best for me in grass are *Crocus speciosus* and *C. nudiflorus*. The former, with a multitude of dark veins, is the bluest crocus I know, and it has a very bright, contrasting, red stigma. It is weak stemmed, however, and some people object to the way the flowers lie on their sides after the first day. *C. nudiflorus* is sturdier and the flowers are quite a rich shade of purple.

There is one other grass area I have not yet mentioned. It is right at the top of the garden, and was an orchard until the big storms of 1987 and 1990 blew the last of the trees down. I thought it looked so nice as meadow that I decided to keep it that way. I am making it my prairie!

In October 1989, Beth Chatto and I, at the end of a world circuit, finished up in Minnesota, where our friend Cole Burrell showed us around some of the remaining areas of the prairie for which this part of the United States was once famous. Although there wasn't a flower in sight and the air was already cold from the Arctic, we could well see, from the dead remains, what an abundance of riches the prairie flora held. Many of its plants are the antecedents of clones we have developed for our own gardens. Cole was a marvel at identifying everything we looked at. We collected seed and it nearly all germinated excellently. The resulting plants are to form the beginnings of my own prairie. I'm no purist, so I'm adding anything else I like and think will thrive, such as the dwarf pampas grass, *Cortaderia selloana* 'Pumila'.

EARLY SUMMER

The freshness of this season still includes as much promise as fulfillment, which is the happiest state to be in. Self-sowing campanulas and moon daisies join the yellow gentian, Gentiana lutea, *with rodgersias behind and a Hybrid Musk rose, 'Cornelia', behind them. Columbines are everyone's favorite, especially photographers'.*

Early summer mix

THE TWO perennials that speak to me most strongly of early summer are lupines and oriental poppies. 'What about bearded irises?', you may well ask. Sad to say, I have grown out of them. Their flowers are wonderful, but for inclusion in mixed gardening they have too long and obtrusive a nonseason. They will not tolerate shading and cannot therefore be masked, and their foliage is a martyr to fungal spotting. Peonies are as bad.

The peppery scent of lupines is one of the great joys of their June season, and all those spires are certainly inspiring. But they look terrible with mildew from midsummer on, so I treat them as biennials (see pages 64-69).

—— *In praise of poppies* ——

Poppies are different, for the reason that when they have finished flowering you can cut the plants down to the ground. They have no objection to this treatment, need to make little or no growth for the rest of the summer, and they can therefore have other plants – such as annuals or, perhaps, cannas – planted among them and close to their crowns in late June for a summer/autumn display.

I feast on the brilliant scarlet coloring of the common oriental poppy. Just surrounded by the green foliage of later-flowering perennials it is perfectly satisfying. But I do have other ideas for it. For instance, as a companion in the High Garden for dense clumps of purple *Iris sibirica*. In another spot, it has *Clematis recta* 'Purpurea' behind it, the young foliage of which is rich purple and makes a good background.

Left of this grouping is, currently, a large bush of *Cistus × corbariensis*. That quickly makes a handsome evergreen shrub with neat, wavy-margined leaves (bronze in cold weather). The small white flowers open in crowds from pink buds – a new crop every June morning. Easy come, easy go. Any shrub making bulk as quickly as this cannot be expected to enjoy a long life. Behind it, and mainly covering a 'Comice' pear on chestnut supports, grows *Clematis orientalis* 'Bill Mackenzie', some of whose strands stray forward into the *Cistus* and coincide with its flowering at the start of the clematis's own season. That lasts well into October, and its bright yellow lanterns later overlap with the silky seed heads.

To the left of the clematis is a harmonious combination on which I am frequently congratulated, though I fear it occurred without my express intention. The hybrid musk rose 'Buff Beauty' has a dusky (I would say dim) day lily, *Hemerocallis* 'Pink Lady', growing around its stool. I should really make the effort to replace it with a day lily of more definite coloring. Around the corner from here (the borders of the High Garden being

Damp border
The main ingredients in this north-west-facing border (below) are hostas (a prey to snail damage), rodgersias (seen in flower and disregarded by pests) and the herbaceous Euphorbia palustris, *which flowered in late spring, but colors yellow in autumn.*

Self-appointed
Opium poppies (Papaver somniferum) *and* Campanula persicifolia *(above), in blue and in white, are at their best in June. On shedding their petals, the poppies prove irresistible to visitors, who snap off the seed pods.*

———— • ————

Cottage-garden medley
A sunny border in the Barn Garden in June (right) shows opium poppies, foxgloves, the hardy magenta Gladiolus byzantinus *(an excellent filler), and double, white, sweetly scented dianthus. At the front there's a brilliant cranesbill,* Geranium sanguineum *'Shepherd's Warning', with* Euphorbia stricta *behind.*

In full sun
Another part of the border (left) shown on page 53, but looking the opposite way. Prominent is an early-flowering biennial verbascum that I originally collected when on a visit to Transylvania (now part of Romania). Also early flowering within its genus is Lavandula stoechas, *the so-called French lavender, and a showier form of it with longer stems and a prominent purple topknot of bracts called 'Pedunculata'.*

———•———

Season of cranesbills
Many hardy geraniums are flowering in early summer (right). In closeup (below) is the bloody cranesbill, Geranium sanguineum, *into which a head of* Allium christophii *has found its way.*

constructed on a cross) is a rather garish red and yellow combination that I adore: the deep blood-red poppy 'Goliath' (which has a wonderfully stiff, upstanding habit to 4ft/1.2m) with the semidouble field buttercup, *Ranunculus acris* 'Stevenii', of the same height. The reason this is not as crude as it sounds is that the poppy is crimson rather than scarlet and the buttercup's flowers are quite tiny, not big and blowzy like its partner's. If both were large and both brilliant in their primary colors, I might have qualms – or I might not, depending to some extent on what grew around them, how fed up I was with gray skies and other such relevant matters.

I am told that I should call my giant, crimson poppy 'Beauty of Livermere', but I bought it years ago as 'Goliath' and the name suits it so much better. I also have it near the middle of the Long Border, without much in the way of flowers around it, but with a background of cardoon foliage, large, glaucous, and deeply cut. That works well. I later interplant these poppies with cannas.

—— Self-made display ——

The High Garden has a lot of early-summer-flowering stuff, so I will finish it off. Near to the yew archway is a cottage garden free-for-all with magenta *Lychnis coronaria*, slightly paler *Geranium rubescens*, and the china blue or white bells of *Campanula persicifolia*, all of these self-sowing. The corms of *Gladiolus × recurvus* 'Robinetta' multiply so freely and are so easily, if inadvertently, moved around that it, too, has a self-sowing appearance. Its color is cherry red, so a double, dwarf (6-ft/1.8m) *Philadelphus* makes a good contrast with its trusses of scented white blossom. And the big, gray leaves of *Hosta sieboldiana* 'Elegans' are an effective coolant.

In the Barn Garden, the south-facing border under the (molting) shingle-roofed barn is pretty lively, largely with self-sowns – opium poppies, campanulas, foxgloves, lychnis, and sometimes an early-flowering biennial mullein I collected in Romania, with smooth green leaves, but that sets little viable seed, so its appearances are erratic.

Of perennials, there is *Lavandula stoechas* at the front, already flowering in May, and its showier variety 'Pedunculata', which, on longish stalks, displays purple flags prominently above its flowers. The pure white *Dictamnus albus* grows behind these. I greatly prefer it to the purple-type plant, which you find in the wild (I have seen it in Hungarian woodland clearings). The pale green, flanged seed pods are handsome, too, and I like to have fun with them in July, setting light to the invisible oily vapor that collects around them at the end of a hot, still day.

At the back, but flopping forward – everything in this border leans forward because the southwest wind, having struck the barn, comes back off it at much increased speed – is the soft pink *Rosa alba* 'Celeste', whose healthy foliage has a gray cast. At the other end of this border, I have planted in contrast the day lily, *Hemerocallis* 'Corky', and the loosely double, pale blue form of meadow cranesbill, *Geranium pratense* 'Plenum Caeruleum'. The day lily makes up in numbers for the smallness of its flowers, which are bronze outside but quite a light shade of yellow within. The partner to this is *Hemerocallis* 'Golden Chimes', which I have on the other side of the Barn Garden. It is a deeper shade, orange rather than yellow, and the mauve spikes of *Stachys macrantha* are in front of that. I think the two flowers go well together.

Odd couple
Lychnis coronaria *(left) sowed itself in a quite unsuitable spot in a damp shady border, next to* Rodgersia pinnata, *whose flowers deepen to dusky red as they age.*

In the Long Border, the big rosy-mauve globes of *Allium christophii*, extending their range from year to year, are at their best in June, and I especially relish them where they peer through the lowest branches of purple-leaved *Cotinus coggygria* 'Rubrifolius' (syn. 'Foliis Purpureis'). At the border's front, there is a great display of the giant chive, *Allium schoenoprasum* 'Sibiricum'. Its pinky mauve, scabiouslike heads vary a little in color from clump to clump, as all were originally from seed. The young foliage of *Spiraea japonica* 'Gold Mound' shows up well on a quite diminutive bush. The colony of *Libertia peregrinans*, whose leaf color I comment on in my Winter Scene chapter on pages 144-47, adds small white flowers, which are partially hidden by its leaves, to its contribution.

Easing themselves onto the path are cushions of the magenta *Geranium* 'Russell Prichard', which will flower from May to October, and *Osteospermum ecklonis* 'Prostratum', whose wealth of white daisies opens to the sun and is at its most prolific in early summer but keeps going at a less frantic pace later on. All forget-me-nots are pulled out and nasturtium seedlings take their place.

— Gold and silver backdrop —
At the back, golden elm and silver willow (pollarded) are at their freshest, and to the right the double white lilac, *Syringa vulgaris* 'Mme Lemoine', reaches its peak at the turn of May and June. Its habit is so stiff and gawky that I give it a hard pruning every few years. A shrub like this is a complete passenger throughout the rest of the summer and autumn, so I keep it mainly from sentiment but try also to mitigate its dullness with a plant going through it of a Virginia creeper (*Parthenocissus inserta*). This colors well in the fall but it is fiercely competed with for food and moisture by the lilac's greedy roots. Then, next to the lilac and on either side of the border's cross path, is a group of *Eremurus robustus*, 8ft (2.3m) tall and carrying striking long spikes of blush-white stars, late in May. That's quite a drama.

In the border's top section, above the cross path, I enjoy myself most of all. I do believe this is the most successful area, though less photographed than lower down, because the house cannot be fitted in as a background. But then, I don't have to see the house all the time; I know it's there.

Phlomis fruticosa, the Jerusalem sage, carries tiers of hooded, dusky yellow flowers above gray foliage in June. That

Antipasto
The Long Border's main season (left) has still not started, but these contributors will none of them detract from that. The campanula (front) is self-sown but is a welcome, if uninvited, guest.

Late of its kind
Most of the Montana group of clematis have finished flowering by the time this one (above), normally known as Clematis chrysocoma, *comes into flower, with each bloom prominently presented on a long stalk.*

Copy cat

Taking a hint from one of Graham Stuart Thomas's books, I have grown a blue-leaved hosta, 'Buckshaw Blue', in front of Rodgersia pinnata, *my form of which has panicles of pink flowers (left). The Hybrid Musk rose 'Cornelia' is flowering at the back, while in the narrow border in front the globe-shaped heads of* Allium aflatunense *rise above the 'Tartan' strain of biennial stocks.*

— • —

Pop-up bulb

In the Long Border, there's a lot of Allium christophii *(right) pushing through the fresh green foliage of a herbaceous indigo,* Indigofera kirilowii, *whose spikelets of pinky mauve pea flowers tend to be swamped by leaves on my heavy soil, where it grows a little too luxuriantly. Here,* Geranium × riversleaianum *'Russell Prichard' is starting its long season, which runs from late May to the end of October.*

shrub has been with me since 1949, and it has become threadbare, but I can grow things in the gaps. Toward the end of that period, the domed heads of scarlet *Lychnis chalcedonica* contrast with the purple spikes of *Salvia × superba*. The red is strong and pure, but not difficult to accommodate. I only wish it lasted longer. It is helped by cardoon foliage behind. Left of the salvia (which flowers for a long time and has a second crop in September) is the bronze *Helenium* 'Moerheim Beauty' and then a colony of pink *Alstroemeria ligtu* hybrids. Behind them, but flowering a little earlier, is the 4ft (1.2m) *Iris orientalis*, better known as *I. ochroleuca*, and that name describes its yellow and white flowers. Mulleins beyond the alstroemerias are perennial *Verbascum chaixii*, and biennial *V. olympicum*, with crosses between them. Some folks think the mulleins don't go well with pink alstroemerias and phloxes. I do. Near the bottom of the Long Border is rather a nice channel of magenta, deep purple-centered *Gera-*

Deceptively entwined

The everlasting pea, Lathyrus grandiflorus, *appears to intertwine with the species rose,* Rosa moyesii *(left). Though quite close to one another in the Long Border, the pea is actually draped over a purple-leaved berberis. The pea is a thug, with an invasive rootstock, and I knew this when I took it on.*

nium psilostemon running back to the soft pink honeysuckle, *Lonicera × americana*, grown on a pole. Here also are *Clematis recta* 'Purpurea', again 6ft (1.8m) tall and needing the securest support to keep it upright, *Gillenia trifoliata*, whose white flowers dance like gnats, and, holding all together, *Euonymus × fortunei* 'Silver Queen', which took 30 years to mature. Magenta spikes of *Gladiolus byzantinus* surround it.

— Glowing in the dark —

Shade-lovers, like hostas, rodgersias, and ferns, are looking pristine with their young foliage. *Hosta* 'Buckshaw Blue' contrasts well, in the Barn Garden, with the purple, palmate leaves of *Rodgersia pinnata* 'Superba', and those of a stronger-growing clone, as yet unnamed, with only slightly paler leaves and flowers. These last are pink and make a splendid show, continuing in beauty right into autumn, as their tone gradually darkens to sultry maroon.

Among such plants I grow martagon lilies, with a special preference for the albino form, whose yellow anthers contrast with the white Turk's caps. Hardy orchids can be interleaved. At one time, I had a large colony of *Dactylorhiza elata*, with reddish purple spikes, but somehow let it dwindle. These things happen if you relax eternal vigilance. Welsh poppies and the apricot candelabrums of *Primula bulleyana* are other ingredients, as are the very special *Paris polyphylla*, in which leaves and floral parts are green, but most beautifully constructed like spokes on a wheel. In October, the seed capsule splits to reveal brilliant orange seeds.

Structural shrubs

IN EVERY GARDEN there should be shrubs that slowly develop character and grow into beautiful, satisfying shapes giving year-round pleasure. There are many examples that I must not go into here, because I do not grow them myself. Others, I do grow, but they are still at a relatively insignificant youthful stage.

The sort of shrubs I do not mean are lilacs, roses, escallonias, and buddleias. The presentation of the flowers is interesting but the shrub itself has virtually no shape. Elders are coarse trees/shrubs, but are so transformed when every young branch is lined with creamy-white corymbs that I value their temporary structure in its early summer season. In case they don't find an appropriate slot in another chapter, I bring in here my two favorites, deviations from *Sambucus nigra*.

'Laciniata' has elegantly cut leaves and larger flower heads than average. They pile up into a great festal soufflé confection, and this tree/shrub looks well behind my hedge of 'Penelope' roses. 'Purpurea', my other favorite, should now be 'Guincho Purple', we are told. The purple coloration of its foliage is projected into the inflorescence. Although the corolla itself is white, the stamens are purplish and so are the subtending pedicels. Its generous swags of blossom seem to epitomize early summer.

— *Fundamental framework* —

However, I must now turn to the more seriously structural elements. At the center of the High Garden, where the cross paths intersect, there is a spire of *Chamaecyparis lawsoniana* 'Ellwood's Gold'. Now a sizable feature, it looked a ridiculous pygmy when it was first given to me more than 30 years ago. The gold of the title is barely apparent, though there is just a hint of it on the young shoots.

On the opposite corner, there is an evergreen couple that pleases me, though its days are numbered. It is made up of a substantial lump of *Hebe cupressoides* 'Boughton Dome' with, behind it, a strong yet graceful spire of *Abies koreana*, a silver fir noted for producing cones as a youngster – if you get the dwarf strain, that is. Mine is far from dwarf, and the only time it attempted to cone, the effort was nullified by an April frost. However, as a slim young tree, I like it a lot. When it outgrows its position, I shall get rid of it and plant another, there or elsewhere. Itself, it is the second in this series of replacements. I

Ubiquitous laurel
The 'Otto Luyken' clone of cherry laurel, Prunus laurocerasus *(below), plays a leading role in almost every public or institutional planting. I value the strength of its compact, upright habit, further reinforced in spring by candles of blossom.*

believe in enjoying a shrub, particularly a conifer, in its youth, even while knowing that it will inevitably outgrow its welcome in a limited number of years.

The hebe is a witch's broom that Valerie Finnis spotted on the typical species in a Scottish garden. She propagated it from a cutting and it is now a widely popular shrub in this dumpy form. It gives off a delicious cedarlike aroma.

I have *Hebe cupressoides*, itself, either side of the steps leading down to our Sunk Garden. My father had clipped box bushes here. In their 30 and more years of life, my hebes have become gnarled, misshapen, and obviously long in the tooth, but their personalities appeal to me – and I pay no heed to the advice of tidy-minded friends.

On the four corners of the Barn Garden, and overlooking the Sunk Garden, are four clipped bushes of the evergreen *Osmanthus delavayi*, now 40 years old. I would not call them structural, however. They have

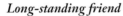

Long-standing friend
I have been enjoying this non climbing ivy, Hedera helix *'Conglomerata' (left), for the past 40 years. It weaves in well with winter-flowering heathers. Low, slanting sunlight gives 3-D depth to its upright spikes.* Iris foetidissima *is paired with it.*

no shape other than that imposed by clipping, which is done immediately after their April flowering. They would have even less structure if unclipped, but they do make firm corner pieces and their scent on flowering carries 100ft (30m) or more on the air.

In these positions my father originally had *Yucca gloriosa*, which is really structural and a true architect's shrub. Not a mother's choice, however, for fear of their needle-pointed leaves spearing her children. The yuccas went soon after my father's death. However, I do grow *Y. gloriosa* in two varieties. 'Nobilis' is a less stiff clone and less severe, with the bluish bloom overlaying its leaf surface. That flowers pretty regularly in the Barn Garden, and I have other strap, or sword, leaves nearby: phormiums and dwarf pampas grass. A dwarf cardoon and self-sown *Eryngium giganteum* (Miss Willmott's ghost) tie in well, and there is a unifying carpet of golden creeping Jenny, *Lysimachia nummularia* 'Aurea'.

I have *Yucca gloriosa* 'Variegata', with a bold cream variegation, on a prominent corner of the Long Border, "making a statement," as they say. I wish it would remain as a single, symmetrical crown, but on building up to a certain strength every yucca crown has to explode into flower. There follows a long, unsightly period, during which all the leaves in that flowered crown die, being eventually replaced, usually, by two young rosettes arising, so to speak, from the ashes.

One of the finest structural shrubs is the evergreen *Fatsia japonica*, with its great, glossy, fingered leaves. That grows in a

Conifer corner
On conifer corner (left), in the High Garden, the spire of Abies koreana *puts on 24-28in (60-70cm) in height, annually. I realize there is no room for a tree here, but why not enjoy one in youth, then yank it out and plant another if I feel like it? The mound of* Hebe cupressoides *'Boughton Dome' has the attributes of a conifer, even to the extent of an aromatic, cedarlike odor.*

Four of a kind
On each of the four corners of the Barn Garden (right) I have a specimen bush of Osmanthus delavayi, *a small-leaved evergreen kept to its rounded outline by being clipped over, annually, immediately after its April flowering. Its heavy fragrance at that time is carried a great distance on the air. Clipping stimulates new growth, on which the next spring's blossom is borne.*

cool border in the Wall Garden, with a back tapestry of the large-leaved, variegated ivy, *Hedera colchica* 'Dentata Varie-gata'. This it has largely obliterated but, as I write, I see that my fatsia is faltering. I may have to cut large portions of it (currently 8ft/2.3m tall) hard back. Because I like to see the ivy as a background, this severe treatment won't worry me un-duly. The fatsia's spreading habit allows me to underplant with a range of shade-lovers – in particular, ferns, hostas, Welsh poppies, and snowdrops.

— Stylish evergreens —

Some of the ivies are quite structural in their own right, espe-cially when grown as bushes propagated from adult material and having no propensity to climb. The one I like best in this respect is a bush of adult *Hedera canariensis* 'Gloire de Marengo', which is handsomely variegated. Mine grew 5ft (1.4m) tall and more across, but was then killed by a hard winter. I replaced it with one of its own children from a cut-ting, and that is now becoming significant. Its greatest moment is in late autumn, when covered with flower buds.

Near to it on the lower terrace is an unusual-looking ever-green shrub, *Trochodendron aralioides*. I shall have to find out whether it will stand being cut back. Now some eight years old, it is 6ft (1.8m) tall but gaining 12-14in (30-35cm) a year and it can grow to 30ft (9m) even in England, and twice as high in its native Japan. Its leaves are oval, pale green with paler margins, unusually thick, and as smooth as soap. They are arranged in clustered whorls with a length of bare stem beneath. Its flowers, in May, are green, borne in panicles and showing prominent stamens like wheel spokes.

Nearby grows *Daphniphyllum macropodum*, a most satis-factory evergreen shrub, now 9ft (2.8m) tall, and in need of re-juvenation, I have to admit, though I have my doubts about its reaction to a hard cut-back. Its leaves are rhododendron-like, and it is often mistaken for one, but they are smooth and silvered on the underside. They are borne in clusters and hang downward in winter, at which time the leaf stalks are a bright and cheerful pink. This is a distinguished-looking shrub of surprising hardiness.

I have become the increasingly proud owner, in recent years, of a holly planted in the High Garden, where it is now 6ft (1.8m) tall but only 14in (35cm) across at the base. This is *Ilex aquifolium* 'Hascombensis', with very small, neat leaves and near-black stems. It seems to be putting on 14in (35cm) of growth annually, now that it is in its stride. So many fastigiate trees and shrubs have a clumsy branch system, but this one has great potential in small gardens where lateral space is re-stricted. The most stylish evergreen shrub in my garden is *Euonymus × fortunei* 'Silver Queen', in the Long Border. It is extremely slow-growing, but therein lies the style, which can only be gradually developed. It must be 35 to 40 years old, now, and is 4ft (1.2m) tall by twice that width. Each branch, densely set with tiny branchlets, has its own personality and is clearly separated from its

Slender and shapely
The hybrid Magnolia × loebneri *'Leonard Messel' (right), while growing quite quickly, retains a narrow columnar habit, clothed with twiggy branches right down to ground level. The impact of its flowers is heightened by an absence of foliage at the time.*

Slow to mature
The most beautiful shrub for all seasons in my Long Border is the evergreen Euonymus × fortunei *'Silver Queen' (right). It has taken some 30 years for it to attain its present size. At one time I thought it would never reach forward as far as the path. But slow-growing trees and shrubs, provided they remain healthy, are those that assume the most beautiful shapes in the long run. There is only a small amount of green in the center of each leaf. The broad margin is pale yellow in spring, when young, maturing to white. In a climate with hotter summers, this shrub would produce berries freely, but we can enjoy ten days, each May, when it seethes with tiny, cream-colored blossom.*

neighbors. If you want quick results, go for 'Emerald Gaiety', which makes a satisfactory specimen quite rapidly, but style eludes it. 'Silver Queen' has a white marginal variegation on a pale green leaf. In young foliage, the variegation is pale yellow. Later, it seethes with tiny blossoms, which the bees love. In my climate, you may get a few colorful spindle berries but nothing like the crops seen in New England.

It is the strange property of *Euonymous* x *fortunei* and its cultivars, of which 'Silver Queen' is no exception, that as soon as they find themselves near to a vertical surface – even a notice board will do – they become self-clinging climbers. Yet you seldom see them grown in this way.

It should not be thought that only evergreens are structural. *Cotoneaster horizontalis*, for instance, is all structure based on a fishbone arrangement. These fishbone branches stand outward, like brackets, when growing, bird-sown, on top of our retaining walls. Or, against a wall face, they rise in curves when they hardly require any support.

Although my specimen is young as yet, I shall write of *Cornus alternifolia* 'Argentea', one of the prettiest shrubs/ trees, with horizontal branches that rise in tiers. Its small leaves are white and green, light and airy. *C. controversa* 'Variegata' is of similar habit and construction. I like it slightly less because of its larger leaves. They flush rather too early and are often mauled by an April frost.

— *Shapely magnolias* —

Some deciduous magnolias are beautifully shaped. Our *Magnolia denudata*, an end piece at the bottom of the Long Border, was very slow growing but took on a Japanesy shape, with a twisting trunk crowned by umbrella branches. Unfortunately this part of it died. *M.* x *loebneri* 'Leonard Messel' has been a much greater success in its ten years with me. Now 10ft (3m) tall, it has made a shapely column of twiggy branches right down to ground level and without any pruning other than those I have cut for the house. Its stellate flowers are a definite shade of pink, and they open over quite a long period. If some are damaged by frost, others will replace them.

Another *Magnolia* x *loebneri*, the white-flowered 'Merrill', makes a fairly shapeless lump of a shrub unless it is pruned to a more elegant shape, as Keith Wyley does in the Fortescue Trust's garden in Devon, where he prunes it to a broad-based spire. The job is done at midsummer, and does not then diminish the next spring's flowering.

Contrasts in form
The only conifer in the Long Border (above) is the slow-growing Pinus mugo. *Marking a corner, just in front of it, is the stiff and spiky* Yucca gloriosa *'Variegata'. At the end of the year, you can usually see clearly which are your most trustworthy plants in terms of long-lasting qualities of shape, color and texture.*

Just visible at the back are two skeletal plants: the grass Miscanthus sinensis *"Silver Feather", which has quite bleached since its September flowering, and a teazel,* Dipsacus sylvestris, *that grows wild in nearby woods and appears when they have been coppiced. It dies after flowering.*

CULTIVATING
Magnolias

The flowering of magnolias, with their pink, purple, or white (like *Magnolia denudata*, here) goblets in early spring, is heightened for dramatic effect by the fact they have not yet come into leaf. Most magnolias dislike lime. At Dixter, our soil is fairly neutral, so there is no problem. If yours is a borderline soil and your plant's foliage is yellowish in hue, annual waterings with iron sequestrene will often put things straight. What magnolias most resent is any disturbance of their fleshy roots. However, quite large magnolias can be moved if necessary, but this should be done in spring. Then the plant is ready to right the shock by immediately putting out new roots. An autumn or winter move too often results in damaged roots simply rotting.

Biennial display

FROM SEED to flower and back to seeding again, biennials take two growing seasons to complete the job. Most of them make a great display in early summer and I love them for that. So does everyone else; what they dislike about them is the unsightly remains, or (if these are pulled out) the gap they leave for the rest of summer and autumn, after they have flowered. That doesn't worry me because I'm prepared to be ready with replacements for them, like cannas or late-sown annuals.

—— Changing combinations ——
I raise some of my biennials deliberately, while some are self-sown. Foxgloves and mulleins come into both categories. The foxglove, *Digitalis purpurea*, that I most often sow is called 'Apricot' and I want it all in that color. It looks good in the Long Border with early-flowering perennials like *Allium christophii* and the everlasting pea, *Lathyrus grandiflorus*, with the wine-red flowers of *Rosa moyesii* and the gray foliage of *Salix alba* 'Sericea'. It flowers too early for the border's main season but I replace it in early July with something like *Cosmos bipinnatus* 'Purity' (from a May sowing). These foxgloves, grown for a purpose, are sown in a pot in April, pricked out into a seed tray, then lined out in the vegetable garden till the autumn. There they make enormous plants, bigger than self-sowns could possibly be but easily transplanted to a border position (or potted into large pots for display in front of the porch) in October-November.

My favorite biennial mullein is *Verbascum olympicum*, with a 7ft (2.1m), branching candelabrum of yellow flowers. That is at its best in July and it flowers rather too late for fitting in re-

Devils and ghosts
Love-in-a-mist, Nigella
damascena *(right), becomes*
devil-in-the-bush when its
horned seed pods develop. It is
an annual, but the largest plants
develop from overwintered seedlings.
Eryngium giganteum *is popularly*
known as Miss Wilmott's ghost,
maybe because this grand Edwardian
lady was pale and prickly?

placements. 'Arctic Summer' is good for its rosettes of silvery leaves in the first year. The flowering spikes tend to twist all over the place, but are amusing in their way.

Every few years, I indulge in sweet williams, *Dianthus barbatus*, again from an April sowing, and lined out for the summer. They don't start flowering till June but lend themselves to being interplanted with tulips. Last time I grew them I followed with May-sown petunias. Tulips are normally associated with wallflowers, *Cheiranthus cheiri*, but because these make pretty scrawny plants, I prefer to pack them close together and group my tulips behind. You must grow wallflowers yourself from seed if you are to have decent plants. I like to sow, outside, in May and then line out the seedlings. Erysimums can be treated in the same way, but should be sown a month or six weeks later, otherwise they flower too much in their first year. Siberian wallflowers belong here, and there's a mauve-flowered species, *Erysimum linifolium*, that is fun to use with late tulips.

Mystery mullein
Most of my mulleins, such as
Verbascum olympicum, *reach their*
peak in July, but the one whose yellow
candelabrums you see here (left) is
more than a month ahead. I brought
a seedling back from Transylvania,
in 1981, but have never known
its name. Foxgloves are no
mystery. They are everywhere and
more seedlings have to be pulled
out than left to flower.

———•———

Mainly for foliage
A dramatically highlighted
candelabrum (right) against a
shadowed background should not
disguise the fact that this mullein's
main attraction is in the silver-gray
of its foliage rosettes. 'Arctic Summer'
is one of several seed strains of
Verbascum bombyciferum.

Special seed strain
The soft, restrained coloring of Digitalis purpurea 'Apricot Beauty' (left) has been attained, and must be retained, by rigid selection and subsequent isolation from the original pinky purple foxglove. If I saved my own seed, mongrels would result.

Happy returns
I return to sweet williams (above) every two or three years, bedding out a good block of them, like the rich red one seen here. Their season being June/July, I interplant with tulips for early interest. Then, late in July, the whole area is replanted.

whose globes of mauve flowers on 2ft 6in (70cm) stems bloom in May. I also grow these with seed strains of border carnations such as 'Tige de Fer' (iron stem). There are quite a number of seed-raised perennials like this, which never give a better display than in their first year, so I grow them as biennials and discard them after their flowering.

Border carnations flower in July but, before then, their glaucous foliage makes an excellent setting for earlier flowers, such as those of the allium, and for tulips. For example, *Tulipa praestans*, whose own foliage is glaucous but broad, where the carnation's is narrow, looks most seductive, its scarlet blooms opening to reveal a black center.

Lupines, anchusas and hesperis

Lupines make excellent biennials from a spring sowing, being subsequently lined out. They'll flower in their rows a little in autumn, and you can rogue out those you consider inferior; then lift and bed out the remainder. Their young foliage is delightful as a setting for rosy red 'Halcro' tulips.

Blue anchusas, *Anchusa azurea*, are best treated as biennials. Being 3ft (90cm) tall at flowering, each plant requires the support of one cane and a twist of unobtrusive soft string. You can raise them from seed, like lupines. Then, on planting them out, I take the bits of fleshy root that break off and treat them as root cuttings, plunging them somewhere well drained for the winter. When they shoot in spring, they are lined out.

Finally, sweet rocket, *Hesperis matronalis*. I prefer the white-flowered seed selection to the mixture that is mainly mauve, and I sometimes fill the two rather shady beds in our topiary garden with just these, the old cow house (called the hovel) being their background. They flower at 5 to 6ft (1.2 to 1.8m) in May to June, which leaves plenty of time for a summer replacement.

May-June flowering stocks, like Brompton and East Lothian, are sown the previous July or August and I take a chance on them, but they are not altogether hardy and are much easier to bring through cold weather in light soils than in my clay. If I see them being attacked by botrytis, they are sprayed with a protective fungicide. The scent of stocks is worth working for, over as long a season as possible. There is a single white variety (it has colonized cliffs in the Isle of Wight) of greater hardiness than most, and it can be quite long-lived. I interplanted it with bulbous sparaxis, which are a good deal hardier than their reputation allows, and that was colorful. With a biennial strain of stocks I currently have *Allium aflatunense*,

SOWING
Biennials

Many biennials are self-sowing and in private gardens we are glad to let them do so. But the best results, both for quality in color and for size of plants, are achieved by deliberate sowings under controlled conditions. The timing needs to be right. Foxgloves, mulleins, Canterbury bells, sweet williams, and wallflowers (*Cheiranthus cheiri*) seldom bloom at half-cock in the first year, so they can be sown in spring. This gives them time to make large plants for bedding out in the autumn.

Siberian wallflowers, biennial stocks, and hound's tongue (*Cynoglossum amabile*) are only too ready to flower if sown early; July or later is best for these, as for certain dianthus.

Treat 'em rough
Anchusa azurea (seen with a head of Allium christophii) is a tall, border perennial but it is so much at its best in the first year from seed that I throw it out after its initial early summer flowering.

HIGH SUMMER

Early morning suits this season, before the flowers (especially verbascums and roses) have become tired, limp, and crumpled by the heat. But that is rare in England's climate. Here the Long Border is stretching itself, the scent of phloxes strong on the air. Clematis are at their peak, including 'Victoria' and 'Bill Mackenzie'.

High summer color

WHEN NIGHTS as well as days have warmed up, we can most enjoy being in the garden. In the hard, flat light of noon, the flowers may look limp and the scene unattractive, but this is amply compensated for in the cool of evenings and mornings. Many gardens concentrating on shrubs are virtually finished by the second week in July, when the once-flowering roses have faded. But, with the emphasis on annuals, and tender and hardy perennials, I have always preferred to look beyond, and, indeed, right to the end of October.

— Flocks of phloxes —

Phloxes are a favorite perennial with me. They love my heavy soil and I love their heady scent and ample duvets of voluptuous color. I write of *Phlox paniculata* in its many manifestations. The wilding itself, from which they all derive, comes from the United States, and Margery Fish gave it to me together with the white form, *alba*, which is slightly shorter. I grow them one behind the other in the Barn Garden. *Phlox paniculata* is mauve, 5ft (1.2m) tall, and requires some support. The flowers are small but light and airy.

I like them best in a planting at the lower end of the Long Border. There they are backed by purple *Clematis* x *jackmanii* 'Superba', which is partly supported by a pole and partly by a tall, September-flowering privet, *Ligustrum quihoui*. To the left of this is the golden cut-leaved elder, *Sambucus racemosa* 'Plumosa Aurea', hard-pruned each winter for best foliage effect. In front of that, and to the phlox's left, are white spikes of *Verbascum chaixii* 'Album'; to its right, a favorite day lily,

Hemerocallis 'Marion Vaughn'. This is moderately late-flowering and presents its lemon-yellow flowers as though each were seeking my attention, individually.

I have colonies of phlox all along the border. Of few do I know the name, because they have been acquired from friends or were a part of the scenery before I appeared. The great point with phlox is that they should be healthy and vigorous, and of colors that I like. Never mind whether the individual pips (as flowers are referred to in this context) are large and well formed, and suitable for the show bench. I don't care a rap about that, but I do care that they should be free of the dreaded leaf and stem eelworm (more correctly known to Americans as nematodes). That is something that can be judged by seeing them growing in someone else's garden before they come to me.

The next group of phloxes going up the border is made up of a lilac-mauve one that was "always" here. Behind it, I have the deep indigo-blue aconite, 'Sparks' Variety'. In front, I

Spikes and spheres
The spikes of Lysimachia ephemerum *(right) arise from a clumpy, 3ft (1m) tall plant of cool, blue-gray foliage. It likes moisture, whereas* Allium sphaerocephalum *grows wild in dry meadows. But I have put them together. Such is the way of gardeners.*

GROWING
Japanese anemones

Anemones as a group have a freshness that we associate particularly with spring. Japanese anemones are no exception, except that they bring this pristine quality to late summer and autumn. The white-flowered kinds are purer than the pink, given the ideal contrast between white petals, a pale green center and a ring of tiny yellow stamens around that. Their continuity of blossom almost rivals a bedding plant's, lasting in my garden from late July to mid-October. This makes them invaluable as a background to summer bedding, which can be of any color scheme I like but will always look right against the white anemones.

An old friend
I acquired the foreground shrub (right) when working, as a student in my summer vacation, at Wallace's old nursery in Tunbridge Wells. That was in 1949, so it is a good age. It is the Jerusalem sage, Phlomis fruticosa. *Though still healthy, it has splayed outward and become gappy, but that means I can allow things like snowdrops and sweet-scented violets to colonize the gaps. This is the way a border evolves.*

used to have *Monarda* 'Cambridge Scarlet' and that was excellent until the monarda refused to thrive for me any longer in that position. It also became a martyr to mildew, which had never been troublesome before. Following a young friend's suggestion, I am thinking of planting some *Helenium* 'Moerheim Beauty' here. I think its warm brown coloring would stand out particularly well.

In this area, I also have *Campanula lactiflora* 'Prichard's Variety'. It is a mere 4ft (1.2m) tall, compared with a more usual 6ft (1.8m), and it has a deeper campanula-blue coloring than I have met elsewhere in this species.

The next phlox along and at the front of the border is the dwarf, dead white 'Mien Ruys' (which my Dutch friends say should be pronounced Rowss, though one lady insisted on Royce). It has a rather short and relatively early season, so there's not too much of it, but I do enjoy the fun when the neighboring *Geranium* 'Russell Prichard' infiltrates with a spangling of its magenta blossoms.

Above the border's cross path is planted a sizable area of a loud, pink phlox, whose July flowering slightly overlaps its neighbor's, the dusky yellow *Phlomis fruticosa*. Not a happy

A good mix
The mixed planting (above) has Clematis × jackmanii *'Superba' at the back,* Sambucus racemosa *'Plumosa Aurea' by its side, a white mullein,* Verbascum chaixii *'Album', in front, and the mauve* Phlox paniculata *to the right.*

Top of the Long Border
This is the most successful section of the Long Border (right) in summer. Alstroemeria ligtu *hybrids make a group of pink in the center. The spikes of purple are* Salvia × superba, *which goes well with the scarlet domes of* Lychnis chalcedonica.

conjunction, I admit, but brief enough not to necessitate intervention on my part. There's more of the taller mauve phlox behind this pink one, but sandwiched between them I am establishing a white bun-headed hydrangea, which is not unlike a phlox itself. This is *Hydrangea arborescens* 'Annabelle'. You can prune it hard back in winter, almost as though it were perennial, as it flowers on its young wood.

Beyond the phlomis is a very jolly planting, one which, in its variety, I should like to think epitomized my way of thinking. The phlox, pink with a white eye, I call Doghouse Pink, because it came from a friend who lived at Doghouse Farm (originally a pub, The Dog). Highlighting it behind is the rich purple foliage of *Cotinus coggygria* 'Royal Purple'. At the back is another *Clematis x jackmanii* 'Superba' on a pole, with the yellow *Senecio doria* in front and to one side. At 6ft (1.8m), it carries domes of yellow ragwort-daisy flowers, but the leaves are plain and undivided, with a gloss on them as though the plant was wearing a mackintosh.

Jostling spires

Buddleia 'Lochinch', with gray foliage and long, lavender spikes, has a soothing influence but there is nothing soothing about the many yellow verbascums in this area. They tend to self-sow and move around, sometimes jostling against pink neighbors. To my mind, that's great.

Another fairly hectic contribution is made by the giant *Kniphofia uvaria* 'Nobilis' with its fiery pokers (I have a row of this in my nursery area in the High Garden, which is so spectacular that I cannot bear to disturb it, though I cannot claim that it has any pretentions to artistry). By its side are the creamy panicles of *Artemisia lactiflora*, offset by darkest green

foliage. This is a perfectly hardy and self-supporting 6ft (1.8m) tall plant. It loves heavy, moisture-retentive soil, and I am pleased to say it does very well for itself at Dixter. I have three groups of it in this border.

Ringing the changes

It is only a little farther to the very top of the border, and things still look good here. At the back is a large planting of cardoons, *Cynara cardunculus*, which I brought home with me from Wye College (where I was first student and then lecturer) 40 years ago, and have never moved since then. It starts with magnificent gray cut leaves in spring, flowers in August with big lavender-blue thistle heads, crowded over with bees, and finishes in stark skeleton form, silhouetted against the sky. At that stage, I like to see the flower heads capped with snow, if I must have snow at all.

This rubs cheeks with a hard-pruned specimen of *Gleditsia triacanthos* 'Sunburst', whose young, lime-green pinnate leaves have their own maturer green foliage for background. Things keep changing in a border. One never gets it quite right or else, just when it seems perfect, it refuses to stay that way, or I tire of perfection (very easy, that). I want a shrub in front of the cardoons and the gleditsia to form a background for my vivid red *Crocosmia masoniorum* 'Dixter Flame' (my own seedling). Either purple or glaucous foliage would do. I have failed with previous attempts and am now trying *Rosa glauca*. Once it is strongly established, I shall prune it entirely for foliage effect. In front of the crocosmia, and at the border's margin, I have *Houttuynia cordata* 'Chameleon'. In warmer climates and moister soil, this can be a terrifying weed. By giving it a hot, dry position, its growth is moderate and its

A real scorcher
No one can ignore Crocosmia *'Lucifer' (above) in its fairly
brief July season. The question is, what do you put with it? I am
glad when* Lychnis coronaria, *as here, seeds itself nearby,
as its magenta moons are surprisingly effective.*

coloring, with so much sunshine beating on it, as harlequin-hectic in cream, green, and magenta, as I could wish.

Right at the top of the border there are white Japanese anemones. How I love them in their simplicity: a circle of white petals, a ring of yellow anthers, a central knob of green. They start flowering in the last days of July and keep up the pressure until mid-October. My main plantings of this flower are in front of the house and as a background to my summer bedding, which can be of any color; the anemones always look appropriate. I also have a 4 ft (1.2m) tall pink one which I believe to be 'September Charm', both in the Long Border and in a shady corner of the Wall Garden, where it goes well with pink and white hydrangeas.

The Wall Garden is at its most colorful in July and August. In the center of its longest border, there is a burst of new blos-

som, early every July morning, on *Cistus* x *cyprius*: big white disks with a maroon blotch and a yellow flake at the base of each petal. The dark evergreen foliage makes a suitable background and smells deliciously aromatic, but it changes to leaden gray in cold winter weather.

A lot goes on around it. There are two lysimachias. The clump-forming *Lysimachia ephemerum* has cool, glaucous leaves supporting 5ft (1.4m) spires of white stars. Around its feet ramps *L. ciliata*, only 2ft (60cm) tall, its yellow stars soft enough in tone not to quarrel with a nearby pink tree mallow, *Lavatera olbia*. This soft shrub receives a hard pruning each spring (even so, it has to be replaced every four or five years), but it still makes huge bulk, carrying its racemes of showy blossom from early July well into fall.

To the right of that and cloaking the border from front to back, where I give it a hoist on a short pole, is an enormous *Clematis* x *jouiniana* 'Praecox'. It has no climbing devices but is super-efficient ground cover. Its wealth of tiny blossoms, borne in panicles, are skimmed-milk blue, flowering from July to September. As this cloak is a bit featureless, I have broken it with two plants of *Helianthus salicifolius*, grown entirely for its columns of narrow, down-drooping leaves that look more like a papyrus than a sunflower.

To the left of the *Cistus* is a group of *Euphorbia schillingii*, not too well placed, I have to admit. I thought it would grow a little taller. But it is a great introduction (quite recent), clump-forming, not a runner like *E. sikkimensis*, and carrying its bold, lime-green flower heads from mid-July for two months.

— *Border performers* —

At the front of this border grows *Asphodeline liburnica*, a curious species, whose racemes of spidery yellow flowers open only at four o'clock in the afternoon, and then only on fine days. It makes a great welcome at that hour, however, its July season coinciding with the thistly blue heads and metallic blue stems of *Eryngium* × *oliverianum*. There's a patch of *Alstroemeria ligtu* hybrids beyond these, inextricably intermingled with *Hemerocallis lilio-asphodelus* (syn. *H. flava*), both of them runners, but it doesn't seem to matter too much. The yellow day lily has finished flowering long before the pink alstroemeria comes into flower, so there is no clash.

Not true blue
No clematis is true blue but 'Lasurstern' (right) makes a blue impression, more so than in this reproduction. Geranium psilostemon is an exciting shade of purple, almost magenta, with a black center.

In the shadier border that is opposite it, the darkest position of all is occupied by a pink, 4ft- (1.2m-) tall *Filipendula*, which is a meadow-sweet. I find the naming of the different forms of this plant so confusing that I shall not attempt it. We planted surplus stock among the dogwoods near the Horse Pond, and they have learned to cope well in these rough conditions.

My own seedling
Crocosmia masoniorum *is normally orange. From a batch of seedlings, one came red and I named it 'Dixter Flame' (above). You see spikes of* Acanthus spinosus *by its side.*

No depressive, this
Some people dislike heleniums because their rays habitually hang down. But that doesn't make them hangdog. This is Helenium *'Moerheim Beauty' (above), an old variety.*

Inula and poppy heads
Although quite an invasive plant that requires chopping around with a spade each winter, Inula hookeri *(left) is one of my favorite yellow daisies. Its furry buds unfold as a spiral scroll. The rays are fine spun and the disks are a favorite feeding platform for July butterflies.*

SUPPORTING
Asphodeline

Asphodelines have starry yellow flowers, whereas asphodels have white ones. The curious feature in *Asphodeline liburnica* is that its flowers (which are most prolific in early July) do not open till four o'clock in the afternoon, and they go to bed at dusk. But they are there to welcome your return home from work. That is, if it isn't raining, in which case they'll miss out for that day. They look pretty in front of the blue-stemmed *Eryngium* × *oliverianum*. A clumpy, 3ft (1m) tall plant, its stems are weakish and I find it advisable to insert a short stake behind each clump and to pass one strand of fillis from this, around each flowering stem, and back to the cane.

Jekyll and Hyde reversed
The yellowish green flowers of Cestrum parqui *(left) droop in hot sunshine and give off a sour odor to an approaching nose. Late in the evening, all is changed and a delicious almond-flavored aroma emanates from the plant.*

There are two hostas in this border, *Hosta ventricosa* 'Aureomarginata' and 'Tall Boy', both free flowerers, with lavender bells or trumpets. Behind a group of the former, and flowering at the same time, in July, I have quite a colony of *Veratrum album*. In a good year, that is spectacular, but not every year is good. It has a stiff, branching panicle to 5ft (1.4m), along every limb of which are ranged white stars. They slowly fade to green, but the structure maintains its presence. Nearby, in total contrast, is an amorphous heap of the pale yellow *Nepeta govaniana*. If I lost it, I shouldn't mourn. The willow gentian, *Gentiana asclepiadea*, is happy here, where it flowers in August. It weeps forwards, laden with blue funnels along each stem, and I have to pull these back before the colchicums that I planted in front start flowering in the autumn.

— *Arresting eyeful* —

In the Barn Garden, the most arresting feature anywhere, during their limited August season, is provided by a narrow, 25ft (7m) tall column of *Eucryphia* × *nymansensis* 'Nymansay' and, in the same eyeful, an old, 7ft (2m) tall hummock of *Hydrangea aspera villosa*. The eucryphia unfolds its white flowers rather as an emerging butterfly dries and expands its wings. Each flower is full of red-tipped stamens and the bees around this honeypot sound like a factory. They collect pollen from the hydrangea – blue pollen which accumulates into blue sacs on their legs. But while the center of the lacecap inflorescence is blue, the surrounding rim of sterile florets is

lilac. The leaves are rough and hairy so, unlike most hydrangeas, it is often misidentified. The 4ft (1.2m) *Crocosmia* 'Lucifer' can hardly be missed, right across the garden, unless you are habitually looking at your feet, and it's surprising how many people never stop to take in the general scene. There are four bushes, one on each corner, of *Osmanthus delavayi*, which catch everyone's attention in April, when they are smothered with fragrant blossom.

— *Perennials for semishady borders* —

The semishady border, in which I have *Hemerocallis* 'Corky' and the pale blue double meadow cranesbill, has several other good perennials. *Geranium pratense* 'Plenum Violaceum' has neatly formed purple rosettes, flowering slightly later than the blue. Behind it is a rampant yellow daisy, *Inula hookeri*, beloved of butterflies and 3ft (90cm) tall, with finely spun rays that open from a spirally swirling bud and whiskery bracts. To the right of this is a small-flowered purple knapweed (to all appearances), which I got from Bloom's nursery more than 20 years ago as *Jurinea glycantha*, but I find no mention of it in books. It's quite a charmer in its way, so I don't know why it doesn't get around. *Astilbe chinensis taquetii* has a strong presence, and because it self-sows, it is not confined to one area. The crinkly leaves are handsome and the rather narrow panicles, which are 4ft (1.2m) tall, are a strong shade of mauve. I used to contrast them with strong yellow ligularias, but that was a bit much, even for me. (Though my stomach might be stronger now.)

The largest yucca I grow is in this garden, *Yucca gloriosa* 'Nobilis', less stiff than the type plant and with a glaucous bloom over the leaf surface. Its heavy candelabrums of waxy white bells open in July. But I have quite a range of other yuccas, some of them variegated, and they are all more or less willing flowerers in high summer.

The virtues of self-sowers

THE RELAXED FEEL of my garden is largely on account of the numerous plants that have been allowed to remain as self-sowns. Their positions have not been designated; they are self-appointed. As much could, of course, be said of a garden full of weeds, but I must add that my observant eye and restraining hand are necessary adjuncts. In respect of my own body and mind, I have always found that to relax requires more concentrated effort than to strain, and I think it is the same in the garden.

To take opium poppies, *Papaver somniferum*, as an example. First, they present us with their waxy, glaucous foliage on which drops of water sit with the uneasy instability of quicksilver; then, come their shepherd's-crook flower buds, soon to open as a new crop of fragile blooms each morning. The discarded calyx segments sit for an hour or two like overturned boats on the expanding petals before finally being thrown off. Finally come the pepper-pot seed heads which have provided a decorative motif in so much carving: pew ends are known as poppyheads.

My favorite self-sower during its long, July-to-November season is the purple Verbena bonariensis *(left). Its flowering coincides with numerous late butterfly hatches, so a colony of this verbena becomes a lively sight on sunny days.* Helenium *'Moerheim Beauty' is seen behind.*

Seeds are scattered on the wind in their thousands, and many germinate where their presence will inhibit the development of smaller or less fast-growing neighbors. Even where well placed, seedlings will be so crowded they ruin their own chances to develop into handsome plants. Interference is essential at quite an early stage in the development of this scenario. Properly applied, these poppies will look marvelous in the early-summer mixed border, perhaps near other self-sowers as in the Barn Garden, with *Campanula persicifolia* in white and in blue, with the gray foliage and magenta moons of *Lychnis coronaria*, and with the contrasting spires of foxgloves. There'll be shrubs and perennials too; cranesbills, roses, dittany (*Dictamnus albus*). It's altogether a gladdening hodgepodge. I also like them among the big planting of white Japanese anemones that forms a background to summer bedding in front of the house. The anemones are late starters, so the poppies are a welcome bonus to provide color between the spring and summer bedding displays.

— Forms of honesty —

The biennial honesty, *Lunaria annua*, is a bonus in May. I have three strains of this and need to keep them apart in different parts of the garden. The rich purple kind that Miss Jekyll knew and grew is in front of the house. It there consorts with nearly related, self-sowing wallflowers (among the male ferns), and these, in their old age, become virus-infected with stripy flowers, as does the honesty. I pull those.

In the Barn Garden, I concentrate the variegated strain that has mauve flowers above green-and-white-variegated leaves; a charming combination, in my view, but unsettling to

Happy coincidence
The bright yellow bird's-foot trefoil, Lotus corniculatus, *seems to me to make cheerful pools of color on the floor of my Sunk Garden (above), though it is a mere self-sowing weed. It combines excellently with the crimson burrs of* Acaena novae-zelandiae.

Invited guests and gatecrashers
In this part of a normally wet and stodgy border (right) are a couple of perennials that I originally saw looking well together at Sissinghurst Castle. They are a prolific yellow, small-flowered day lily, Hemerocallis *'Corky', and a loosely double form of our native meadow cranesbill, the blue* Geranium pratense *'Plenum Caeruleum'. Foxgloves and poppies have infiltrated among them.*

those who like their colors clean and straight. This strain is a recessive and will come true from seed so long as it does not cross with a plain-leaved kind. If it does, all the progeny will be green in the next generation, separating out only in the generation following that. So I have to be sharp-eyed and remove green-leaved seedlings before they flower.

Handsome umbellifers

The pure white honesty, with the somewhat paler green foliage that is typical of so many albinos, grows on the south side of the house and is the handsomest of them all and excellent to pick and arrange with poet's narcissus (*Narcissus poeticus recurvus*) and the acid lime-green inflorescences of *Smyrnium perfoliatum*. Another favorite self-sower, it prefers a moist, partially shaded position, so it works in well, at the bottom of the Long Border, with Lenten roses (*Helleborus orientalis* hybrids) whose young foliage provides a pleasing background. *Smyrnium* is a monocarpic umbellifer, often mistaken, on account of its structure and coloring, for a euphorbia. It takes at least three years to flower from seed; then sets quantities of shining black seeds and dies. Once you have it established there's no problem in keeping it (or in its keeping itself), but the early years are tricky as the young seedlings disappear completely from sight during the summer and autumn months and can easily be inadvertently removed.

Ghostly intruder

Likewise Miss Willmott's Ghost, *Eryngium giganteum*, of the same umbelliferous persuasion, generally takes three seasons from seedling to flower with me. This stiff, prickly 'sea holly' needs full sunshine, however, if it is to achieve its palest silvery coloring in the ruff of bracts that surround the domed sea-blue flower head. It grows only 2ft 6in (75cm) tall and looks good in its July season with *Lychnis coronaria*, and with the flaming red *Crocosmia* 'Lucifer'. In fact, I have a sneaking affection for all three plants together, magenta clashing boldly with red, but this is not always easy to organize as the lychnis and eryngium sow where they please, which may not be where I please. With its tap root, the eryngium is virtually impossible to transplant. It also goes well in a bed where I have the blue umbels of the late-flowering bulb, *Brodiaea* (now

Triteleia) *laxa*, and, when I plant them in, bright pink *Viscaria* 'Rose Angel' from an autumn sowing, which have been over-wintered in a frame and planted out in early spring.

Spring self-sowers

Early in the year, I should like to have self-colonizing winter aconites but have yet to succeed with them. Common snowdrops self-sow, for instance, among the gnarled stems of my 40-year-old *Phlomis fruticosa* and here also is a colony of white, sweet-scented violets, which seems to have been the first established strain of *Viola odorata* at Dixter. We subsequently brought in the typical violet-colored kinds and the pink, sometimes known as 'Coeur d'Alsace'. They all hybridize in the Long Border and are ideal at the foot of deciduous shrubs, or around the tufts of oriental poppies.

Primroses, mostly the pale yellow wilding, abound in similar positions. Then, in April and May, comes the time of forget-me-nots (*Myosotis*), whose blue haze comprises a unifying theme through most of my borders at that time. I'm fairly strict with columbines, England's native *Aquilegia vulgaris*, but it has a place – and I enjoy it – under the skirts of a *Hydrangea petiolaris*, which I grow as a shrub, not a climber.

I weed out all the bugle, *Ajuga reptans*, in my borders. I used to grow various clones with variegated or otherwise

See-through self-sower
In its second year, Britain's own teazel, Dipsacus sylvestris *(left), develops into a strikingly handsome candelabrum. Though tall, it is easy to see through and past it, as at the front of the Long Border here, to a group of* Campanula lactiflora *'Prichard's Variety'. The teazel's tiny mauve flowers come out in July, after which the plant dries to a fine skeleton, attractive to behold.*

Botanist's misnomer
Whoever named Eryngium giganteum *(right), which seldom grows more than 3ft 4in (1m) tall, cannot have seen E. decaisneanum, which reaches three times that height. E. giganteum takes two or three years from its self-sown seed to reach flowering size; then dies – most unpleasantly. It is seen here in a group of* Coreopsis verticillata, *which have yellow daisies and feathery foliage.*

Two protagonists
This contrasting pair (left) makes a splendid show. The foxglove, Digitalis purpurea, is normally rosy purple, to which it gradually reverts, on self-sowing. But I frequently grow on fresh seed of selected strains. Opium poppies, Papaver somniferum, also revert to a mauve prototype.

Early on the scene
Scented violets, Viola odorata (below), come in a range of colors from violet to white. This pink one was my mother's particular pride. Wood anemones, Anemone nemorosa, arrived more or less by accident, clinging to the roots of other plants introduced from our surrounding woods.

colored leaves, but they were difficult to control, self-sowed untrue to name, got mildew, and were generally tiresome, but the wilding is a charmer with its spikes of blue in spring, on the floor of the Sunk Garden. The biennial *Euphorbia stricta* is welcome both here and in the borders, but the constraint that is imposed on its growth in paving cracks brings out a nice red coloring in its stems, which harmonizes with the lime-green haze of its inflorescence.

Moon daisies (*Leucanthemum vulgare*) have colonized most of the paving cracks on our sitting-out terrace and are a glorious sight in June, though leaving little space for chairs. At the end of the month, they are cut flush with the paving and their vacated space is freed for general usage, though wand flowers (*Dierama pulcherrimum*) make many tufts and flower gracefully throughout July. A recent takeover bid is being made by a New Zealand sedge, *Carex comans*, with 12in (30cm)

tufts of arching brown leaves. The gloss on these gives the lie to rude suggestions that the plants look dead. But I shall now have to reduce their numbers.

Two plants whose seedlings I almost automatically extract at every encounter are astrantias and lady's mantle, *Alchemilla mollis*. Both quickly develop extremely tough and woody rootstocks, so the younger I can dispatch them, the better. The Welsh poppy, *Meconopsis cambrica*, of which we have the yellow and the orange forms in roughly equal proportions, can be a great nuisance – for instance when it self-sows into a colony of low-growing ferns like *Adiantum venustum* – but I have a soft spot for it. How good it looks in May, for instance, among and beneath hydrangeas whose young foliage is so far their only contribution. Again, they make the jam in a sandwich of hostas and vigorous ferns.

—— *Keeping alliums in check* ——

Some alliums are such pestilential colonizers that it is wise to exclude them from the first – I have to be severe even with my giant chives, *Allium schoenoprasum* 'Sibiricum', which makes such a grand display in May, but I try to cut them to the ground before seeds have ripened, which they very quickly do. It's the same story with the pure white *A. neapolitanum*, whose flowered stems I grab between both hands, then sharply tug so that they all break cleanly away from their bulbs. But *A. christophii*, of the big lilac globes in June, is a surprise. It has taken over a large section of the Long Border and I can't say I mind. I don't clear the border of last year's debris till March. In the meantime, the allium's seed heads have blown about and become lodged in some obstacle, where they deposit their seeds, and the tiny seedlings can already be seen when we get around to our annual tidying up.

—— *Large intruders* ——

The large quaking grass, *Briza maxima*, is hung with scaly, green heart-shaped lockets in May-June on 15in (38cm) tall plants. After that it sows itself prodigiously and most of the seedlings must be extracted in the same autumn. Freed of competition, it can make a large plant. Tiresome name changes in the biennial evening primrose, now *Oenothera glazoviana*, make it difficult for the wretched gardener to keep abreast of the times. This grows to 6ft (1.8m), and opens large, bowl-shaped yellow blooms so late in the evening that they would be easily missed but for the fact that they flower on until mid-morning the next day, before wilting. Most of mine are in the Barn and Sunk Gardens, and I like them best of all when they seed themselves in paving cracks. The dead skeletons are a pleasing sight in winter.

Here, and in the Wall Garden, is the home of *Libertia formosa*, with stiff, evergreen, irislike leaves and panicles of white triangular flowers in May. It marched through the brick archway dividing these two gardens, taking the step risers in its stride on the way. This does not make old bones gracefully; there's an accumulation of dead leaves that is hard to remove discreetly. Best, I find, to scrap old plants and allow self-sown seedlings to take over. It looks most effective in the company of *Euphorbia griffithii* 'Fireglow'.

—— *Geraniums and verbena* ——

Several monocarpic cranesbills are free self-sowers, including Englands own herb robert, *Geranium robertianum*, with pink flowers, and I also have a white-flowered strain wherein the calyx stems and veins are red. *G. rubescens* (in the High Garden) is a handsome plant, making a bold rosette of red-stalked, deeply cut leaves in its first year, and carrying deep pink flowers in its second.

But my favorite of all the self-sowns, and the one that does me proudest all over the garden, is *Verbena bonariensis*. This is a 6ft (1.8m) tall plant, whose square green stems make a greater impression than its small leaves. The dense heads of tiny purple flowers are borne on a branching candelabrum. Their season starts in July and gradually builds to a climax in September. Although tall, this is a see-through plant that can be indulged at a border's margin, where it so often puts itself, just as well as in the center or at the back. These plants seldom live more than three years, being at their largest and most prosperous in their second, so one depends on self-sowing for its continuation. In the colder climate in the north of Britain, seed isn't set and this consequently becomes a difficult plant to retain in those areas.

Botanists' playground
This 6ft (2m) tall evening primrose (above) was called Oenothera larmarckiana *when I first knew it, then* O. erythrosepala, *but the latest (don't count on it sticking there) is* O. glazoviana.

CONTROLLING
Leucanthemum

This self-sown moon daisy, *Leucanthemum vulgare* (syn. *Chrysanthemum leucanthemum*), decided to make its statement at the top of Lutyens's steps, overlooking the orchard, where its antecedents originated. Within a few months it had been killed by ants nesting in the crown of the plant. But there are plenty more, in self-appointed spots, including our sitting-out terrace, on the next level up, which is a sea of white in late May and early June, leaving little room for chairs and tables. Order is restored a few weeks later, after we have grabbed at and torn out everything within our grasp. That leaves the roots, so the show will be repeated the next year. The way their flowers follow the sun's diurnal course is typical of many daisies, including sunflowers.

Roses in a setting

ROSES ARE no monomania with me. The bush is shapeless at best, more often downright ugly, and rescued only by its foliage, flowers or fruit. To me it seems obvious that roses need to be integrated with other plants, other themes. That would mean that you could not grow nearly so many of them, which is surely as it should be when there are so many other deserving plants.

Yet I have a rose garden. It was designed by Lutyens in the original plan, and it is prettily shaped, architectural yet not unduly formal. It assimilates an ancient cow shed – the Hovel – and a circular, brick, cattle-drinking tank. The geometrically shaped beds are divided by flagstone paving. It would be difficult to transform into anything other than a rose garden, unless it were something considerably more expensive to maintain. What I should really like would be a summer garden of tropical bedding, cannas in particular, but also an interesting range of other handsome foliage plants, not necessarily tropical but contributing to that mood. It is sheltered here and hot in summer, and therefore the ideal place for them.

As it is, I tend to diversify with other kinds of plants. One of the best effects I have achieved so far is of combining a patch of orange *Lilium pardalinum* with the single shrub rose, 'Golden Wings', which I'm not really fond of but it has the advantage of growing strongly. I much prefer 'Mrs. Oakley Fisher', the cuttings of which were given me from Sissinghurst by Vita Sackville-West. My collection of roses is full of museum pieces. The oldest, brought here by my parents from their first garden (they were married in 1905), and thought by Graham Stuart Thomas to be 'Candeur Lyonnaise', is still as vigorous as you could wish to see, a Hybrid Perpetual with cream-colored blooms, annually throwing up stems some 7ft (2m) tall or more, which I peg to the horizontal.

'Mme Isaac Pereire' also dates from then, though I have layered quite a few of its stems to make more of it. For its scent and for the generosity of its full, double magenta blooms, it is possibly my favorite. Most of the roses I have propagated myself from cuttings, so as to be free of a pestilentially suckering rootstock. 'Peace' is an exception. In the early 1950s, I was experimenting with budding and with making standards from wild rose stocks. That particular rose is still going strong, though it suckers like mad.

Roses and lilies
I am not keen on rose gardens consisting only of roses. Eventually, mine may end by having none at all! At any rate, I am diversifying. The fairly large shrub rose 'Golden Wings' (above) looks good in early July with a group of Lilium pardalinum, *seen here. If your soil is light, roses look wonderful with regal lilies,* L. regale, *known for their scented, white trumpets.*

Up the tree
My Rosa filipes 'Kiftsgate' (left) climbs through a damson tree. It is one of a number of similar, ultra-vigorous, once-flowering white roses, of which 'Wedding Day', 'Toby Tristram', 'Bobby James', 'Rambling Rector', 'Francis E. Lester', and Rosa mulliganii *(which forms a bonnet of blossom in the center of Sissinghurst Castle's white garden) are other examples. They need a strong tree to bear their weight. Pruning them is hell.*

•

Unusual teammates
At their first June flowering my row of the Hybrid Musk rose 'Penelope' is often joined by self-sown moon daisies (right). It is also underplanted with some daffodils. Behind, the tree is Sambucus nigra *'Laciniata'.*

This, and the rest of my roses, are spread around the garden, none of them concentrated to any extent. In the Barn Garden originally there used to be two large beds of the China rose, 'Comtesse du Cayla'. It is not entirely hardy, and most of mine were killed in the 1947 winter, but some remain, and I am fond of them, particularly for their scent. 'Perle d'Or' was given us in the 1930s and one of those original bushes remains in the Long Border. The other, a cutting I rooted from it, greets you as you enter the Barn Garden from the Wall Garden, and it always seems to be at its best at its second (autumn) flowering, when its coloring is a more definite shade of apricot and its scent wafts freely on the air.

That is a virtue in many of the Scotch roses, mutants of *Rosa pimpinellifolia*. They do sucker a lot, but still. . . . Some of the Hybrid Musk roses are excellent wafters, in particular the pale pink 'Penelope', of which I have a short hedge. It has a peculiar history. Originally rooted from cuttings, it lasted for many years but gradually weakened. I decided to have it dug out, and replaced it with other shrubs (*Clethra, Corokia*). But the bits of 'Penelope' root that had been left behind all sprouted and made new, rejuvenated plants. So I'm back where I was, with additives that just have to get along as best they can under the circumstances.

'Felicia' wafts well in the High Garden, and I have 'Cornelia' and 'Buff Beauty' here and elsewhere. A fairly strong bush of 'Frühlingsgold' was given me at Wye College around 1953, when I was lecturing there, by a student, Frank Taylor, who had grafted it himself when working in a nursery. It has never suckered and is still going strong.

— *Aromatic foliage* —

Roses with aromatic foliage that gives off a spicy fragrance appeal to me, and I have three of these. *Rosa serafinii*, a small, twiggy bush with white flowers and small red hips, I grew from seed from one growing in the White Garden at Sissinghurst. I haven't caught its scent without pinching a leaf, yet. Britain's native sweet briar, *R. eglanteria*, continually self-sows. I believe in pruning its flowered wood each winter, to encourage the production of young shoots that grow right into autumn, their young foliage giving off that delicious smell of stewing apples. Old foliage is much less smelly. Then there is *R. primula*, with its extraordinary aroma of incense, which it is reluctant to yield when pinched, but

Richest scent of all
The Bourbon rose, 'Mme. Isaac Pereire' (above), is a winner. Generously repeat flowering, it makes swags of growth. The blooms are crammed with petals (and not a few earwigs) and deliciously scented.

• — •

Gawkiness disguised
Rosa centifolia 'Cristata', known also as 'Châpeau de Napoléon' and 'Crested Moss', has an awkwardly leggy habit, which I disguise by growing it among a mixture of other plants in the Long Border (left). Geranium 'Ann Folkard' intermingles.

On the peg
In two of the Rose Garden beds (below) grow vigorous, cane-making varieties that I lay to the horizontal with strong ash pegs, cut from nearby coppiced woodland. This encourages them to flower along their entire length.

which is so powerful on the air in muggy weather. To my chagrin, I have failed to root this from cuttings, but it does occasionally yield an extra plant from its own suckers.

I love the true Rugosa roses, with their rough-textured, healthy foliage and such sweetly scented flowers. Of these 'Alba' is my favorite, its leaves a fresh, pale green and the globular hips bright orange. Unfortunately these are often gouged out for their seeds by greenfinches. I can't think why anyone should prefer 'Blanche Double de Coubert', whose double blooms nearly always have a moldy patch on them, and whose foliage is nowhere near as hearty.

— *Species roses* —

I have colonies of three American species, all enthusiastic suckerers. *R. woodsii fendleri* is a newcomer and, as I knew it had a reputation for spreading, we enclosed its site with a sheet of plastic sunk into the ground. This was nowhere near strong enough and the rose escaped in its first year! Its single pink flowers are followed by a great crop of red hips. In *R. virginiana*, flowers and hips are of minor importance but its red stems are a winter asset, while the main feature is the varied autumn coloring of its glossy foliage, spread over a six-week season. I believe that all roses should be pruned regularly for renewal, and in this case we cut all flowered growths right out at ground level, leaving only the young wands made in the previous summer. So, too, with *R. foliolosa*, whose forward-pointing, narrow, leaflets are so untypical that visitors often need to be told that it is a rose. It has deep pink, single flowers from July to October, well scented. Of the eight or so different roses I have in the Long Border, the showiest is 'Florence May Morse', which grows to about 7ft (2m) on a chestnut pole. It is a kind of Floribunda, the double flowers not beautifully shaped, but their strong red coloring over a month-long season is invaluable, red in a mixed border always being at a premium in my experience. Roses, bedding plants and tender perennials provide it most obligingly.

Sheltered spot
The site of the Rose Garden (above) was a farm cattle yard. Lutyens designed it to have scalloped yew hedges on three sides and the Hovel (a cow shed) on the fourth, the roses being in a pattern of formal beds. It is very sheltered; stiflingly hot in summer, cold as a morgue in winter.

Diversification
Under shady lengths of hedge on the Rose Garden's perimeter, ferns and hellebores prosper (above). This is the soft shield fern, Polystichum setiferum, as you'll find it in the wild, but it has many cultivated varieties. The Floribunda rose, 'Allotria', is one that I rooted from a cutting.

Quite simple, really

Everyone, including myself, is puzzled by the naming of Rosa 'Complicata' (right), seeing that it has single flowers like a wilding. It is a once-flowering Gallica, but will set a showy crop of late-ripening hips if not dead-headed. Most Gallicas have a tendency to throw suckers from their own roots. If this was likely to be a nuisance in any given position, you might after all be better off with grafted plants, provided they did not sucker from the rootstock.

Rose and fern again

Roses look particularly good against a backdrop of ferns (above). I have rooted most of my roses from cuttings at one time or another; if I take my cuttings quite early, say in June, they will be ready for potting off singly by early August and for potting on in spring.

Rosa moyesii and *R. setipoda* both have long, showy red hips. I grew the former from Royal Horticultural Society seed in the 1930s and was lucky that it came true, as this species crosses readily. So its flowers, in early summer, are deep blood-red. In *R. setipoda*, which I raised from a cutting, they are pink, saucer-shaped, pale at the center, the sepals protruding cheekily beyond the petals. Its hips catch everyone's attention and hang on for a long while.

— Border bloomers —

At the back of the border I have two climbing 'Grüss an Aachen' roses, each on its own pole. This is a comparatively modern rose, yet it has the numerous petals and fullness of older kinds. It is cream with a hint of pink and was raised from cuttings that Lady Birley gave me.

Near the top of the border, and right at the front, I have the polyanthus rose, 'The Fairy'. Its glossy leaves and neat, double, clear pink flowers endear it to me. Then, again, its late flowering makes it fresh when other roses are past their first prime. In August it is joined by a colony of Chinese chives, with heads of white flowers, growing through it.

Right at the bottom of the Long Border, and growing against one of Lutyens's tile pillars supporting the loggia, is 'Irish Elegance', an old friend, even older than me. It is a single rose with coral-colored buds, definitely its best stage. The open flower, sadly soon bleaches.

Hydrangeas

HYDRANGEAS PLAY a strong part in my affections, and in my garden. There is a summery voluptuousness about them that carries right through from early July to late October. I like the fresh smell of the plant, which meets me pungently when I'm pruning in March, or when I'm taking cuttings. And I like their glossy leaves, which squeak as you handle them. There is a generosity in their growth that encourages me to feed and water them – little attentions that they greatly appreciate. On the whole, hydrangeas seem to like me, but I will confess to two failures before going further. I would dearly like to please 'Preziosa', but I insist on having it in a certain part of the Long Border where it tones in with other plantings. But it obstinately refuses to be pleased. 'Lanarth White', a lacecap with pale green foliage, is the other recalcitrant.

It makes little difference to me whether my hydrangeas are lacecaps, in the wild style, or hortensias, with bun-shaped flower heads packed with showy, sterile florets. Both have

Hortensias
Bun-headed hydrangeas (right), in which most of the florets are large, showy, and sterile, are called hortensias. They make a good display, but, as garden plants, their hardiness is often questionable.

Caps and cones
This deep pinky red lacecap, 'Geoffrey Chadbund' (opposite), would be purple on acid soil. Dark coloring goes with dwarfness. Hydrangea paniculata 'Tardiva' has the typical white cone-shaped inflorescences of this species. It is totally hardy and flowers on the ends of its young shoots.

Easy to recognize
The hortensia, 'Ayesha' (below), is unique in having florets that incurve at the margins, rather like lilac flowers. And their surface is highly glazed. It has a long flowering season, but is not very hardy.

their appeal. Neither do I mind too much about their coloring, which can vary so much according to soil acidity. But if they're called Blue something, it does look a bit foolish to see them pink. I have never tested my soil for its pH, but assume that it is fairly near to neutral. Most of my colored hydrangeas are pink or red, rather than blue or purple.

I have attempted to change the color of 'Blue Wave', 'Blue Deckle' and 'Bluebird' from pink to blue, through fortnightly applications of aluminum sulfate from February until flowering and, if persisted in over a couple of seasons, it works. It is a bit laborious, however, and I'm generally quite happy with pink as a hydrangea color. Among the first in flower, at the turn of June/July, are *Hydrangea serrata* 'Diadem' and 'Bluebird', both lacecaps, the former no more than 2ft (60cm) tall and charmingly informal. 'Bluebird' is exceptionally hardy but its season is fairly short. The hortensia 'Vibraye' or, to give it its full title, *H.* × *macrophylla* 'Générale Vicomtesse de Vibraye', starts early but has a very long season and is outstandingly hardy. It normally has buns of small, pale pink florets, but these will be a pretty shade of light blue if you happen to have acid soil.

Mainly for foliage
The American species, Hydrangea quercifolia (left), is a wonderfully bold foliage plant, its oak-shaped leaves changing to deep red in late autumn. It is quite hardy. Cones of white blossom are carried at the tips of second-year branches.

Other long-flowering cultivars of *Hydrangea × macrophylla* are 'Ayesha' and 'Mme Emile Mouillère', which is the best general-purpose white hortensia in my opinion. In bright sunlight, it tends to turn pink on ageing and may scorch brown, but if you remove the early trusses (a branch at a time) as they deteriorate, other young shoots will develop and take their place. 'Mme Mouillère' has a four-months-long season. 'Ayesha', no less, but this is a more tender variety and may have most of its flowering wood destroyed in frosty gardens. Quite distinct from other hydrangeas, its florets are incurved, like lilac blossom, and shiny, like bits of porcelain.

The red coloring that deep-toned hydrangeas produce on my soil is more eye-catching than the purple they turn to on acid fare. Thus the dwarf hortensia, 'Westfalen', is very striking, while 'Geoffrey Chadbund' is the lacecap equivalent.

Hydrangea macrophylla 'Mariesii', at the top of the Long Border, has a rather upright habit, which lends itself to under-plantings with tulips. It comes midway between a hortensia and a lacecap, with flat heads wherein there are large, sterile florets, not just on the rim but scattered through the disk.

— *Different types of hydrangea* —

Completely different in habit and appearance are the varieties of *Hydrangea paniculata*. They flower on their young wood (with the exception of 'Praecox'), are always white, and have conical flower heads. The wilding, from Japan, was given me by Collingwood Ingram, who collected it there from the sides of a volcano, inside the rim of whose crater needle-tailed swifts nest (he told me). This clone has been named 'Kyushu'.

I also have 'Floribunda' and 'Tardiva' (also *Hydrangea paniculata* varieties), between which I can see little difference. Their cone-shaped inflorescences are scattered over with large white florets between the foam of tiny fertile flowers. The size of the inflorescence depends on how hard you prune the shrub. Hard-pruning gives rise to enormous heads, and they are glamorously beautiful. I prefer a rather taller, more lightly pruned shrub. If you get yourself in the right place, sitting on the wall of the lower terrace (just the right height for resting halfway round the garden), the cones of 'Tardiva' seem to be repeated, in the background, by the three white cowls of our oast house.

If you are sitting a little farther along this wall, you are well placed to study the amazing foliage of the oak-leaved hydrangea, *Hydrangea quercifolia*. While most of the hydrangeas we grow originate from the Far East, this is an American species from the mountains of Virginia. Its reputation for lack of hardiness is quite undeserved. The leaves are large and scalloped, like an oak's. The more heavily you prune and feed it, the larger the leaves will be, and as they are this species' salient feature, the sacrifice of its white, conical flower heads is not too serious. In autumn, this foliage changes to bronze.

Mixing them in

Hydrangeas benefit, visually, from being mixed in with plants of different habit (right). At the back are two clumps of the giant reed grass, Arundo donax, hobnobbing with a small-headed hortensia, Hydrangea × macrophylla 'Nigra'. In front, two lacecaps, 'Blue Deckle' and 'Bluebird', have the cranesbill, Geranium endressii 'Wargrave Pink' with salmon-pink flowers, meandering between them. Hydrangeas, naturally are pink or mauve in my fairly neutral soil. To acidify the soil I sprinkle aluminum sulfate granules around their roots, watering well in, every two weeks from early spring until the buds begin to color.

Lacecaps

The wild types of a number of hydrangea species (below) have flat inflorescences, with a ring of showy, sterile florets around the outside and a platform of small, fertile flowers in the center. These are known as lacecaps, to distinguish them from the bun-headed hortensias. There are many named varieties of lacecaps, so it is no use asking the nurseryman for the lacecap hydrangea. He needs to know which one.

The Dixter ponds

I WOULD DEMAND a pond in any garden I owned, however small. At Dixter there are three, and they give me enormous satisfaction throughout the year; at all times, in fact, except when frozen over. Then they die, but that never lasts for long. Soon, reflections and movement are back. The whole ethos of a pond is to teem with life.

When I say movement, I mean the cats' paws of eddying wind over the surface, or the rings of ripples made by swallows as they skim over the water or by fish rising. Unlike many gardeners, I do not like the tinkling of a water spout, with a circulating pump in the background, turned on before the arrival of expected visitors and off when they leave. That's a cheat, and quite different from a natural stream running through or alongside your garden. There are not many of those in Sussex, and anyway, if liable to flooding, they are a nuisance.

When a pond is overhung by trees, the water appears black and there are few reflections. Such is the case with our small length of moat, excavated centuries ago and now heavily

shaded by oaks. The majority of water plants dislike these conditions. Duckweed does not, and a thick green skin of this coats the moat through much of the summer. Flag irises do not mind the shade, and our largest gunnera, *Gunnera manicata*, grows here. The partial shade and exceptional shelter encourage it to make leaves 6 or 7ft (1.8 to 2m) across. Visitors love to be photographed beneath one of these.

I have planted red-stemmed willows along the nontreed side of the moat, and these come to life when struck by slanting winter sunshine. We pollard them every second or third year, because we find that this treatment seems to encourage the brightest stem coloring.

The formal, octagonal Sunk Garden pool was a part of my father's design for this area, made after the First World War. The octagon, be it noted, is not regular, but much more interesting for two opposite sides being longer than the other six. Two stone seat embrasures overlook this pond and, between spring and autumn, I used to enjoy writing my regular gardening articles out here. But now that I write directly onto a word processor, albeit a portable laptop, the light outside is too bright for me to read the screen. Such is progress.

I used to have koi carp in this pond, feeding them twice daily. They were voracious. Carp are great disturbers of any mud in a pond. What with that, and with the murkiness

Misty morning
Where there is water, mists will gather. The Horse Pond (left), in early summer, is slow to rub the sleep from its eyes. The huge umbrella leaves of the Brazilian Gunnera manicata *have barely stretched to their full width – not usually reached until July. Meantime, many plants take advantage of the area around it, which will be quite dark later on, but by then they will have completed their growth cycle. Here are the mauve spikes of the spotted orchid,* Dactylorhiza fuchsii, *which is particularly prolific in the Horse Pond area of the garden.*

Aquatic aroid
Not many aquatics are early in flower, and the golden club, Orontium aquaticum (above), *is among the first, being at its peak in early May. Its flowering stems are straight at first but then take on sinuous curves as they lengthen and sway gently over the pond's surface.*

———— • ————

Bankside bog-lovers
Kingcups (or marsh marigolds), Caltha palustris (right), *form an increasingly dominant part of the landscape the further you travel north in Britain. There, and in western Ireland also, you find the best remaining strongholds of the fern,* Osmunda regalis.

caused by their excrement, and the fact that they bred like fury, you could never see into the pond at all. Since I got rid of them (more than 200, in the end, from an original nine bought from Harrods), it has been wonderfully peaceful, though by no means dull. Natural fauna is not slow to find a pond. There is an abundance of newts, dragonfly larvae, beetles, and much else. The water is clear.

One of my favorite underwater oxygenators flourishes, though it was unable to coexist with swirling fish. That is the water soldier (*Stratiotes aloides*), which forms rosettes of sharp-edged, purplish foliage, of various sizes and seen at various depths. I particularly enjoy looking down into the water at it in winter. A bit of duckweed has moved in since the fishes' departure, and we control this by skimming or raking some of it off once or twice during the growing season. There are bright green rafts of *Cotula coronopifolia*, which covers itself with yellow flower buttons for half the year. The waterlilies (*Nymphaea*) include 'Rose Arey', which is pure pink. Sometimes I buy a blue tropical waterlily, treating it as an annual in its own container, and it flowers from July to October.

It's good to have some verticals rising from a sheet of water. I have the blue *Iris laevigata* 'Zambesi', with the unusual distinction of flowering at any time between June and November. The broadly white-striped grass, *Arundo donax* 'Variegata', also does well under water, but it's cannas that I really long to see in these conditions, as I have, so effectively, in California. I'm still working on that one.

Best of our ponds is the Horse Pond, near to the entrance drive (called the Forstal). It was part of a much larger medieval excavation running back to a steep bank, but up to the time when my parents bought the property it was a drinking pond for the farm horses. It has always been stuffed with fish, and I assume this to be the reason for duckweed never taking a hold.

Time to relax
This is the spot (below) where we spread rugs and drink coffee after lunch whenever the weather permits in summer. In May, the pond puts on a fantastic display from the water violet (actually related to primulas), Hottonia palustris, *which is normally a discreet underwater aquatic, making clouds of bright green, feathery foliage.*

This is the most relaxing area in the whole garden, though you are ceaselessly aware of a tremendous undercurrent of energy and vitality, both in and above the water. Whenever the weather is suitable, between April and September, we bring our coffee out here after lunch, recline on rugs or just on the grass, contemplate, converse, or doze (that's me).

— Secret of success —

There are various contributing factors that make the Horse Pond such a success. Trees are kept in the background. Otherwise they mop up the water disastrously in summer. By and large, the pond banks are steep, often vertical (although the water's maximum depth is nowhere more than 4ft/1.2m), so when the level falls during a drought, it is a long time before mud is exposed. There is always plenty of water surface visible, and this is so important for a pond's enjoyment. Never grow over-vigorous waterlilies. In no time, they take complete charge. Their leaves stand out of the water and nothing else is visible. The five varieties I grow are all in shades of pink or red. They are of moderate vigor, and when their range becomes excessive it is easy to find a market outlet.

The crimson 'Escarboucle' is the most vigorous and, in many ways, the most satisfactory *Nymphaea*, as it is less influenced by weather conditions or time of day, for expanding and remaining open, than any others. Its flowering season is the longest, lasting well into October.

Waterlilies flower most freely in sunlight, but their pads are valuable for providing some shade within the water. This minimizes the affliction of unattractive algal growth, blanket weed and green slime, so common in new ponds that have not yet settled down. Underwater oxygenators also reduce this condition. Many of these, however, are far too invasive, growing too thickly and rising to the surface so that the water becomes invisible. Do be careful what you introduce. With its growth like spring coils, *Elodea crispa* is the most aggressive that I have had to contend with.

My favorite water plant is the so-called water violet, *Hottonia palustris*, actually a close relative of primulas. In the Horse Pond, in winter, it makes underwater clouds of bright, lacy greenery. But in May, flowering stems rise well above the water, the flowers in whorls, like a candelabra primula, white with a tinge of mauve.

— Around the Horse Pond —

This being a natural pond on a clay substrate, the grass banks come right up to the water's margin (the water's highest level is controlled by a piped overflow). Low pollarded willows line the Forstal side, and there is a grove of red-stemmed dogwoods (*Cornus alba*), which look particularly good in winter, and in autumn as their leaves change color.

Gunneras are the largest herbs. Their leaves expand slowly, not casting their deepest shade until July, so all sorts of early-performing plants can thrive among their crowns:

Unbeatable nymphaea
Allowed a depth of a yard or two of water over its crowns, no waterlily will give better value than the crimson 'Escarboucle' (top). It remains open for longer hours and continues flowering till later in the autumn than any waterlily I know.

No passport papers
This giant kingcup (above) flowers quite early. Caltha polypetala was introduced from the Vatican gardens by Reginald Farrer, who hooked it out of a pond with an umbrella handle, while a bevy of aunts distracted the custodian.

99

Restful formality

The Sunk Garden (left), seen in June. The marginal blue-flowered iris is 'Gerald Darby'. In the paving cracks, the crimson pools of Acaena novae-zelandiae *are interrupted by clusters of bird's-foot trefoil,* Lotus corniculatus. *Spotted orchids seed themselves among them.*

———•———

Stoop to sniff

The American Nymphaea *'Rose Arey' (right) is often advertized as being scented. Opportunities for smelling waterlilies are comparatively rare, but when a bloom nudges the Sunk Garden pool's margins, which it does now and again, you can test the proposition. You will discover that it is scented – slightly.*

———•———

Horse Pond inhabitants

Although a weed along the East Coast of New England, the so-called sensitive fern, Onoclea sensibilis *(below), is one of my favorites. It has a running rootstock and is very gradually spreading along a bank. In closeup, you see the flowers of the water violet,* Hottonia palustris.

for example, snakeshead fritillaries, Lent lilies (*Narcissus pseudonarcissus*), windflowers (*Anemone nemorosa*), winter aconites, and wild orchids.

Wild broom seeds itself into the steep bank and makes gorgeous pools of yellow in early summer, the blossom weight dipping their branches into the water. Marvellous reflections. Earliest flowers are provided by kingcups, particularly by *Caltha polypetala*, a large-flowered east-Mediterranean species, as happy in shallow water as on the bank. A little later, but in 12in (30cm) deep water, flowers the golden club, *Orontium aquaticum*, which makes a satisfyingly regular dome of yellow-tipped white clubs.

Native flag irises come in a rush of yellow at the turn of May and June. To these I have added the purple and white *Iris versicolor*. Summer flowers then take over, the waterlilies especially. I do love 'James Brydon', with its deep pinky mauve, bowl-shaped blooms. It is very prolific in July but with a comparatively short season. I grow arum lilies on a submerged island. Each flower will last for three weeks as long as the weather doesn't turn too hot. If it does, they will scorch. In their case, a little shade would help.

Autumn tints are surprisingly warm and then, during the winter months, we can see the water as an almost uninterrupted sheet. That is a truly splendid sight.

Annuals and bedding without beds

ANNUALS, AND the kind of bedding plants that need to be lifted and protected in winter, strongly appeal to me. Their colors are mainly bright and cheering. They can be used in different ways each year or they can be given a complete rest. Mistakes are quickly rectified and forgotten. With trees and shrubs, you need to think rather hard in advance whether your choices are the right ones, because, if wrong, the upheaval is arduous and expensive. Indeed, if the tree has reached a certain, not very large, size, you may need to get the local council's permission to remove it. You are no longer your own master (if you ever were). With annuals, there can be no such objections.

Biennials are in the same case; they have their own chapter (on pages 64-67) as do the kinds of plants mainly used in containers (on pages 112-17). For the rest, I do not like the kind of beds that look self-consciously like beds, often cut out of a lawn in squares, oblongs and circles. For this to work you need to have a highly artificial setting, like Versailles, or Blenheim Palace. Most of us do not!

— *Integrating annuals* —

Plants are plants; we categorize them only for our own convenience. The natural treatment for annuals and bedding plants is much the same as for hardy perennials, bulbs and shrubs. They will all integrate splendidly in mixed borders.

Still, I do have greater concentrations of annuals in some areas than in others. My biggest, L-shaped bed is viewed across a small lawn, bang in front of the house. It is backed by brick walls. The front half is entirely devoted to bedders, changed twice a year; occasionally, if I'm feeling extra energetic, even three times. For instance, tulips and wallflowers could be followed, in June, by a vivid display of mesembryanthemums or nemesias. Both these annuals are out and over in six weeks. They can be swept aside and followed, at the end of July, by nasturtiums, say, from a June sowing, individually or in pairs, in 3½in (8cm) pots. Or by bedding dahlias from an early May sowing and moved into 5in (12cm) pots so that they are budded up and ready to flower by the time they're needed. Busy lizzies would be suitable, as would heliotrope, if only there were a well-scented seed strain. 'Marine' looks okay, and as it develops slowly, an early April sowing will work out right, again moving the seedlings on to final 5in (12cm) pots. Nonstop tuberous begonias make an excellent show,

Poppy and daisy
This prickly poppy, Argemone grandiflora (right), is particularly beautiful on the first day of opening. Its leaves are gray. Sometimes plants do manage to survive the winter and do a second term of duty. It also self-sows a bit. The South African daisy, Osteospermum hyoseroides, is a true annual. It flowers only in the mornings.

Asters take their turn
I always vary my bedding in front of the house (left), and in this year grew China asters, Callistephus sinensis, in a strain called 'Matador'. When you experiment, you make mistakes. I shall not grow this one again because, although the flowers are a nice shape and there is a good range of colors, the plants are top heavy. After a shower of rain, the whole lot swayed sideways in a variety of drunken attitudes, never to right themselves again. Most of us can do better than that.

They grow together
The purple Nigella hispanica *(above), an annual, grows beside an anonymous pink daisy. The latter, half-closed in this picture, has foliage remarkably like a dandelion's, except for being grayer. "If that was in my garden, I should weed it out", is the sort of comment I hear from visitors. But they change their tune when it comes into flower.*

———•———

Versailles and all that
I was trying out this modern seed strain of the familiar Cosmos bipinnatus, *called 'Versailles' (left), and certainly the blooms were large and handsome on the finest plants. A small percentage of the plants are apt to make a lot of growth during summer and to start flowering only in autumn, but they bear the largest blooms. Behind is a late-flowering aconite,* Aconitum carmichaelii *'Kelmscott'.*

not too big and blowzy, but a lot more exciting than the fibrous-rooted kinds. Tubers overwintered in a cool cellar or similar place can be held back for quite a while. Eventually, they can be brought on in moist peat in a closed sun frame, then potted individually, first cutting them into smaller pieces if stock needs to be increased. Finally, out they go. Biennials, like sweet williams, can be followed in the same way.

I should mention that all my plants are brought on or raised from seed in cold frames, without any artificial heat – a method I have found cheap and effective over many years.

To return to that bed or border in front of the house: it doesn't look like a bed because in its back half there is a huge permanent planting of single white Japanese anemones. They flower from late July to mid-October and are a suitable background for any colors I care to use in front. In two central places, the anemones are interrupted by a triangle of *Cornus alba* 'Elegantissima' bushes, which flutter in green and white through the summer months. Their carmine stems look nice in winter, and then I prune them hard back late in March.

In the year that the photographs for this book were taken by Steve Wooster, I bedded China asters, *Callistephus sinensis*, in front of them. The year before, it was a yellow and white scheme with dwarf bedding dahlias (too dwarf for my liking), corn marigolds, annual daturas, prickly poppies (*Argemone grandiflora*) and some variegated succulent *Agave americana*, turned out of their pots in the greenhouse to their great joy –

freedom at last. It was all a lot of fun, though the more vigorous tended to swamp the less so, as the season progressed. It is rarely that I carry out the same idea twice.

There are bits of bedding in the Barn Garden, though because of their mixed surroundings you probably wouldn't recognize them as such. In one corner, I have bedded out currently white penstemons (planted in the autumn and taking a chance on a mild winter) interplanted with tulips. When the tulips have finished, I shall replace them with a summer bedder, possibly *Salvia coccinea* 'Lady in Red', which might contrast rather well with the penstemons in late summer, provided the latter have enough staying power. Young plants usually have. But in the previous summer Steve photographed a combination that pleased me very much: a purplish blue, 2ft (60cm) *Ageratum* 'Blue Horizon' with *Lonas inodora*, an annual reaching a similar height with heads of yellow buttons.

Not far from here, on corners either side of an exit leading to the front path, spring bedding may be combined with early summer bedding, sweet williams being interplanted with tulips. Currently I have red pomponette daisies and tulips here for the spring. Often I follow with a petunia whose seed I originally got from Hungary, where I admired it, in 1981, for being so much less highly developed than the current American F1 products. They have a nice spreading habit and a delicious scent at night. I have been saving my own seed since then.

— *Exotic additions* —

I use quite a lot of cannas in the Long Border, *Canna indica* 'Purpurea' being the most prolific, with fairly narrow, upright leaves. It grows to 6ft (1.8m) and has small red flowers. *C. iridiflora*, on the other hand, has broad, green leaves and, late in the season, deep pink flowers on arching stems. One year I had a lot of stock of *C. musaefolia* which, as its name implies, has immense bananalike leaves, purple around the margins and along the veins but otherwise green. It grows to 8ft (2.3m) in a season and, although it never flowers, it creates a splendid

The brighter the better
The pot marigold, Calendula officinalis *(above), is naturally brilliant orange, which is the way I like it best, though more timorous (or tasteful) gardeners gravitate toward the lemon and "art shades." It flowers quite early, when there's a lot of green around. With it, I grew the gypsophila-like, white* Omphalodes linifolia, *whose foliage is gray.*

— • —

After the lupines
This piece of bedding (right), in the High Garden, follows on lupines. As they're not out of the way until late June, the annuals are not sown till early May, but they grow quickly in the warm weather. Tithonia rotundifolia *'Torch' has rich orange flowers, while* Cosmos bipinnatus *'Purity' is a tall, all-white strain.*

Quite a surprise
Normally only 2ft (60cm) tall, Ammi majus (right) is a popular cut flower in Holland and Germany. I had never grown it well until this year, when I potted self-sown seedlings up in the autumn and planted them out in spring. They shot up to 6ft (1.8m) tall.

Successful experiment
Annuals (below) allow me the pleasure of experimenting with unfamiliar combinations, but without prolonged punishment if things go wrong. I had never grown the yellow Lonas inodora *before. I planted it in front of* Ageratum houstonianum *and hoped that I hadn't got my heights wrong. I was lucky on this occasion.*

Hedge drapers
My self-sowing nasturtiums, Tropaeolum majus *(left), all have this annual's naturally climbing habit. Where they grow close to a yew hedge, they make a colorful curtain against this dark background.*

effect. I planted it among bushes of 'Golden Wings' shrub roses in the Rose Garden, also adding the purple-leaved castor oil plant *Ricinus* 'Carmencita', which is maple shaped, and they were far more exciting than the roses.

Ammi majus is an annual that I grew to perfection in the Long Border one year. In the previous year, I had a row of it in the vegetable garden for picking. It grew only 2ft (60cm) tall but self-sowed that same autumn. I potted up some seedlings, overwintered them in a cold frame and planted them out in the spring. To my astonishment they grew 6ft (1.8m) tall – umbels of pure white with a wonderful lightness. I thought that these would self-sow in their turn, but, to my sorrow, not a single seedling turned up. With gardening it does often seem to be a case of feast or famine.

I do have one bed cut out of the topiary lawn, but its contents are so informal that I hope you would not think of it in conventional terms. This was the site of a topiary yew that fell sick and was scrapped. Instead I have planted a fastigiate, yew like conifer, *Cephalotaxus harringtonia* 'Fastigiata'. There is a lot of space around it, now mainly taken over by blue, self-sowing love-in-a-mist, *Nigella damascena*. Another self-sower that goes well with this is the annual *Calceolaria mexicana*, with lemon-yellow pouch-shaped flowers. The corn marigold,

Chrysanthemum segetum, is good, too, and I have sometimes added the blue, yellow-eyed South African daisy, *Felicia amelloides* 'Santa Anita', which I keep going for the following summer from overwintered cuttings.

In the High Garden, two strips of border where I frequently treat seed-raised lupines as expendable biennials offer great opportunities after the lupines have been thrown out, which is not till the turn of June-July. So the second display reaches a peak in September-October.

It's an ill wind

I struck a good summer for my purpose in 1990 when the drought admirably suited zinnias. Behind them, I grew the annual yellow *Rudbeckia* 'Green Eyes', also listed as 'Irish Eyes', with large daisies on a 3ft (90cm) plant. You need a cane to each plant and a stout cane for *Tithonia rotundifolia* 'Torch', a close zinnia relation that quickly rises to 5ft (1.4m) in suitably warm weather. Sometimes I work in the stately *Nicotiana sylvestris* with this. It has bright green paddle leaves surmounted by a candelabrum of long-tubed white trumpets, deliciously scented at night. The flowers die brown on the plant and need pulling off each time you're passing. In this particular photographing year I had tithonias contrasting with *Cosmos bipinnatus* 'Purity' (which makes a far superior, bushier plant than the much advertized 'Sonata'), with red 'nonstop' begonias in front. These were set against an attractive background of *Miscanthus sinensis* 'Purpurascens', with its ever changing color through the seasons, and with the red fuchsia hedge in the distance.

Places for ferns

ERNS GIVE a feeling of lightness and luxuriance to the garden. Sometimes they are protagonists, at others they provide a supporting cast. Often they infiltrate, unbidden. Their minute spores are carried for many miles on air currents. When they land on some congenial surface, there a fern will grow, and you may well wonder how on earth it arrived.

Wall rue is a case in point. It grows in the rotting mortar of old walls, and nowhere else. No sensible person ever tries to cultivate the wayward *Asplenium rutamuraria*; it just arrives when the time is ripe. When I was a child, the one place it grew at Dixter was in the short stretch of wall on the east side of the Wall Garden, which was the only surviving bit from pre-Lloyd/Lutyens (1910). The mortar in Lutyens's own brickwork is now decaying, however, and wall rue has found its way up to our highest chimney stacks.

The common male fern, *Dryopteris filix-mas*, is our commonest garden fern. My mother planted a border of it beneath the overhanging eaves of the Great Hall's northeast front. She reckoned that a cool ribbon of green was more suitable here than garish bedding. The latter is concentrated in a border

across a lawn and is seen from, rather than with, the house. Most of these ferns have remained undisturbed for the past 80 years, and they have sown themselves into suitably shady spots along other bits of wall. In one stretch I am attempting to replace them with a close relation, the golden-scaled male fern, *D. affinis* (whose name refuses to settle down; we have also known it as *D. borreri* and *D. pseudomas*). Not only are the scales on the young fronds a brighter color in the spring but the frond itself is lime-green.

A ferny bank that I am quite proud of (always remembering that we are in the drier east of England, where the climate is less suited to ferns in general) overlooks the drive on your left as you approach Dixter and is the remaining north-facing exposure of an ancient quarry. It is thick with self-sown ferns, mainly common male and broad buckler (*Dryopteris*

Foliage to the fore
In a shady bed in the Wall Garden (below), ferns grow happily with ivies, honesty (Lunaria annua), here running to seed, and hostas. I underplant them with snowdrops, which like shady conditions, and if the fern fronds are evergreen, as here, I cut them down in time to give the bulbs a breather.

In their different aspects
*Yet another setting (above) for the
fern* Polystichum setiferum,
*which is unfailingly photogenic.
Likened to croziers, the unfolding
young fronds have an animal-like
energy. 'Bevis' was discovered by a
farm worker in a Somerset hedgerow,
more than a century ago, and given
to a keen amateur fern enthusiast.*

Good companions
*I like these three plants together (left).
The fern is* Polystichum setiferum
'Pulcherrimum Bevis', *in which the
fronds are drawn to fine points at the
tip. Then there is a* Spiraea japonica
'Goldflame', *whose young foliage is
coppery, fading to lime-green. At the
back is a lively grass,* Miscanthus
sinensis 'Variegatus', *with
white leaf margins.*

dilatata), which we deliberately avoid when cutting the grass here. The existence of a feature such as this depends on management, otherwise brambles overtake it.

I am always collecting ferns without any such intention, but just because they are irresistible. Where then to place them in the garden becomes the next problem. One of the most satisfactory ways to choose a site is by spotting a self-sown male fern that has discovered a likely pitch on which to thrive, and replacing it with one of my acquisitions. If it was right for one fern, the chances are it will be right for another.

The hart's-tongue ferns, *Phyllitis scolopendrium*, on the other hand, most often place themselves in, or at the foot of, a

Confusing names
The biennial we call honesty, Lunaria
annua *(seen here with* Polystichum
setiferum, *again), would not be
recognized by that name in other
countries, which is why it is so
much safer to use the* lingua
franca *of botanical Latin
with which to
communicate. This excellent
intention is scuppered by the
botanists, who are constantly
altering their view of
what the correct names should be.*

Lime-lover

The hart's-tongue fern, Asplenium scolopendrium (below), is particularly happy where alkaline mortar rubble has broken away and gathered at the foot of walls or steps. It is evergreen and becomes one of the garden's strong features in winter, when other plants have been cut down. Here, it is with our old friend, lady's-mantle, Alchemilla mollis, another self-sower and apt to make itself a bit too comfortable.

Versatile fern

The common polypody, Polypodium vulgare (above) is one of England's most widespread native ferns. It can be a bit stodgy, but is a lot of fun when, for instance, it completely takes over a roof or makes a fringe along a horizontal tree branch. It is very accommodating and will thrive in dry as well as moist shade. It has given rise to a whole host of interesting variants, of which this crested one is an example. Polypodies remain fresh all winter. Spring is their only off season.

wall. They are great lovers of alkaline mortar rubble. With its plain, undivided frond, the hart's-tongue is in complete contrast to the complex divisions in most other ferns. The statement it makes is bold. It conveys its strongest impression in a ribbon along the foot of the old piece of wall I have just mentioned. The plants that form this are all self-sown, and you do not notice them in summer because of the taller border contents in front. In winter, these are cut down and the fern comes into its own.

Normally, the contrast that a fern's leaf form requires to highlight it must come from some totally different kind of plant. Bergenias and hostas, with their plain, rounded leaves and a preference similar to ferns for moisture and shade, are excellent companions bringing out the most in ferns.

Besides male ferns and hart's-tongues, the English species of which I make most use is *Polystichum setiferum*, the soft shield fern. It is just about evergreen, inasmuch as the old

Under the larder window
The ferns (left) under this north-facing part of the house were all self-sown. They are the male fern, Dryopteris filix-mas, which, being deciduous, allows plenty of other incident among its crowns. Snowdrops are quickly followed by scillas (Scilla bithynica). Then the spurge, Euphorbia amygdaloides robbiae, and in August, the willow gentian, Gentiana asclepiadea.

Shades of green
The fresh green, lacy fronds of Polypodium vulgare 'Cornubiense' *(above) contrast with the maple leaves of* Kirengeshoma palmata.

fronds are dying off only as the new are unfurling in spring. At that stage, or even a little earlier, it is sensible to cut the old fronds away, as their tarnished appearance does not provide a very flattering frame to the unfurling young croziers. Also, I tend toward heavy interplantings of snowdrops with my shield ferns, and they'll need to be seen, and to see the light themselves, from January on.

— Surprisingly adaptable —

Polystichum setiferum has given rise to a great many beautiful mutations, of which I have several. Most important to me are 'Acutilobum', which emphasizes two corners in the Wall Garden, and the elegant 'Pulcherrimum Bevis', which makes arching fronds on which the pinnae close forward toward the tip, as though each feather had been dipped in a moistener. That grows under the fatsia, whose own leaves could hardly be in greater contrast; also in blazing sun in the Barn Garden, where the shrub that originally shaded it died. The change hasn't worried my fern in the least. Plants are often more adaptable than we suppose.

The same thing happened to another fern in this border, where a tree peony that was shading *Blechnum tabulare* (syn. *B. chilense*) died. This South American fern has dark green, leathery leaves, tactilely satisfying when drawn through your hand. But in youth, they are coppery and then pale green. As young fronds are produced throughout the summer, the

contrast in color between youth and maturity is most interesting, and it is greatly emphasized in a sunny position. In shade, the fern grows two or three times as tall.

This is a colonizing, carpeting fern. For cultural purposes, most ferns can be categorized as either carpeters or as fairly tight clump-formers. Of our native ferns, the most typical colonizer is polypody, *Polypodium vulgare*, a curtain of which inhabits the top and face of a retaining wall in the shadiest corner of the Barn Garden. Polypodies have many variants, and my favorite is 'Cornubiense', with more dissected leaves than the type, but also the brightest, most cheerful green coloring, which it wears throughout the winter. It goes well with the marbled spear leaves of *Arum italicum* 'Marmoratum' (more familiar as 'Pictum'). I grow two hardy maidenhair ferns, both of which I have seen in their native woodland habitats. *Adiantum pedatum*, from British Columbia, Canada, has fronds of the greatest delicacy, their branches describing an

Double take
A few weeks separate the taking of these two pictures (below and right), wherein a soft shield fern, Polysticum setiferum 'Acutilobum', fringes the intersection of two paths. Welsh poppies are followed by Campanula persicifolia and opium poppies. Although the fern is evergreen, we cut it down in January to make room for giant snowdrops.

For all seasons
These crested polypody fronds, Polypodium vulgare 'Cristatum' group (above), are as fresh in winter as in any season. They acquire their new fronds in June and that is the time to extract last year's crop. A spray of winter jasmine, Jasminum nudiflorum, keeps them company.

arc about a curved semicircular base (the same fascinating structure as you find on *Helleborus foetidus*, the stinking helle-bore, and *Dracunculus vulgaris*, the dragon arum). This species is deciduous and the young fronds, which start to unfurl as early as March, are almost pink. They scorch in hot sunshine and I have served my colony ill by having it in the sun's full glare. I mean it to be shaded by a shrub on its sunny side but have so far failed to find the right shrub.

Adiantum venustum makes a low, evergreen carpet. That comes from the hills in Kashmir. In frosty weather, the green turns to bronze and looks, perhaps is, dead, but still looks good. A notable addition, of recent years, has been *Onychium japonicum*, spores of which Alan Leslie, a botanist friend, brought back from China (it has a wide distribution in the wild), eventually giving me a plant. This is a carpeter, with extraordinarily finely dissected fronds, creating a bright green haze for much of the summer.

I have two ferns in a perfectly open situation by the Horse Pond. It took 30 years for the royal fern, *Osmunda regalis*, to begin to look properly at home, but in the last few it has grown much more strongly. At Scotney Castle in Kent, it grows 4-5ft (1-1.5m) tall by the moat. I wonder how they do it. In spring and early summer its pale, lime-green coloring picks it out at a great distance – a thrilling sight in its Irish haunts. Again, in autumn, it stands out in bright rufous brown.

The other is the sensitive fern (sensitive to early autumn frosts, that is, but ultra-hardy), *Onoclea sensibilis*. That is a weed in New England meadows, where it has to be cut as we do bracken, to check it. I wish it was a weed with me. In twenty years I now feel it to be safely established. Perhaps in another twenty . . . . The fronds are but once divided into quite simple pinnae but their freshness in spring is unbelievable. It would do better in a damp, shaded border, but I want it by the pond. It only needs to get the message.

Pots and sinks

THE MOBILITY of pots with ornamental contents is their greatest asset. My main use for them is in two groups, either side of our entrance porch. There they are a cheerful welcome, when I go in, and wave me an affectionate, sometimes reproachful, good-bye, as I exit. Reproaches are not too often on my conscience, because in their noticeable position they get more attention than plants in any other part of the garden.

The pots are nearly all of clay, which I like the look of and being heavy they are the less inclined to blow over. On the other hand, if they do, they often crack or break. The loam-based composts with which they are filled are also heavy. When their contents are growing strongly, we give them a liquid feed every fourth day.

The porch avoids the worst of our prevailing winds, except in spring. There's sunshine only till mid-morning, which is not, in my experience, warm enough to prevent oleander buds from dropping prematurely, but doesn't seem to affect adversely most of what I want to display. In fact, it actually seems to favor the ferns and begonias. So I kick off in spring with pans or half-pots of small things, like the prolific, early-flowering trumpet daffodil, 'Tête-à-Tête'. *Anemone blanda* looks good, especially the extra vigorous 'White Splendor'. I also have a mauve

strain of it, originating in Tuscany, of *A. hortensis*, which is a true wilding, whatever its name might suggest to the contrary.

— *Pleasing subjects for pots* —

Liliaceous plants that are heavily susceptible to rots and to slug damage on my heavy soil have a much better chance when pot grown. So I grow the April-flowering *Fritillaria pallidiflora* this way. Its bells are palest green.

In a deepish bulb pot, the bulbous *Iris bucharica* is excellent with glossy leaves and flowers in two shades of yellow. Jonquil and Triandrus-type narcissi are also pleasing pot subjects, and I like to mass some hyacinths and early-flowering tulips in quite large containers. Bright colors (including white) to cheer us up are more important in early spring than carefully thought out harmonies.

In May and June there are several annuals that make excellent pot specimens if sown the previous late summer or autumn. Viscarias are most striking in the 'Rose Angel' strain, though a mixture is good, too, the pale blue kinds resembling flax. I generally prefer blue cornflowers to the mixed shades. Cornflowers can grow embarrassingly tall but 'Blue Diadem' comes out about right at approximately 2ft 6in (75cm). With them, one year, I had the corn marigold, *Chrysanthemum segetum*, which is bright yellow. Neither flower is big and blowzy, so the contrast isn't at all crude.

Masquerader
I ordered the January-February flowering Crocus chrysanthus 'Snow Bunting', which has a delicious scent. This odorless late flowerer (below) was incorrectly sent under that name. It is coinciding with the flowering of the hyacinth 'Delft Blue'.

Three chums
The plants shown (above) are three that I often plant in four, more-or-less matching pots around my Sunk Garden, along with a vivid red or orange-flowered 'geranium'. Mignonette, Reseda odorata, smells good from the adjacent stone seat. Lobelia richardsonii is a blue-flowered trailer, while the gray-leaved Helichrysum petiolare is one of the most popular of all trailing bedders in Britain.

Outside my porch
Begonia haageana *(left) is a good windowsill foliage plant. B.
'Flamboyant' is tuberous-rooted and rests in winter. In front
is* Scaevola aemula.

Safest in a pot
*Bulbs that are the particular delight of slugs are safest
grown in pots. Flowering in April (above), is* Fritillaria
pallidiflora, *while* Tropaeolum tricolorum *climbs up behind.*

— Cotoneaster associates —

There's a *Cotoneaster horizontalis* to the right of the porch, and it's fun to have something climbing into it. In spring, it's *Tropaeolum tricolorum*, which starts its climb on pea sticks and goes on from there. Although it isn't fully hardy, it is hardy enough to bring out from cold glass by early April. Its swags of pixie-hooded flowers are rich red, almost black on the rim, and yellow inside. In late summer, I have *Codonopsis forrestii*, a herbaceous twining climber with blue saucer-shaped flowers. You can see the relationship that it bears to campanulas.

Later on, China asters, from an April sowing, are good, using a widely branching strain like 'Ostrich Plume' or the single-flowered types. And *Salpiglossis* are excellent, getting

just enough protection from the house to prevent them going into a mush after hail or heavy rain, as happens in the garden. If you spot any trouble from botrytis setting in, you can pinch out the affected shoots. There are certain muddy shades that I dislike in this flower, so some plants have to be discarded for this reason, but obviously this can only be done when they have started blooming.

— Elegant lilies —

The lily season starts in June and is most important. Of the upright, flowered hybrids, I have a particularly bright orange one that I like a lot, but as it was supplied to me as *Lilium* 'Pirate', which should be mahogany, I don't know its true name. For scent, I like the 'African Queen' strain, in dusky fawn shades. Later, any of the *Lilium speciosum* hybrids. The rank smell of *L. auratum* is also welcome when met outdoors. Finally, there is *L. formosanum*, with elegant white trumpets, purplish on the outside, switching its fragrance on in the evening. It is usually at its best in September and is easily raised from seed, even carrying its first bloom in the same

Cornfield weeds on display
Both cornflowers, Centaurea cyanus, *and corn marigolds,* Chrysanthemum segetum *(left and below) make the largest plants from an autumn sowing. Eventually they can be moved into 7in (18cm) or 8in (20cm) pots and will flower from May on. Regular dead-heading is necessary in an exposed position like this. Lilies give body to the display.*

year. In the second year, I pot three seedlings into each of a number of 7in (18cm) pots.

In a fairly low container, the semicascading *Begonia sutherlandii*, with masses of pale orange blossom over a long period, looks good combined, either in the same container or in one placed near it, with the felted, lime-green foliage of *Helichrysum petiolare* 'Limelight'. 'Flamboyant', an old begonia with smallish, rich red single flowers in great profusion, looked magnificent with the prostrate near-blue (always a wretched color when photographed, alas), tender perennial, *Scaevola aemula*. For its large, reddish, felted leaves, I like to have a background plant of *Begonia haageana*, which spends most of its year on the dining-room windowsill. As I rarely feed it, this looks a trifle peaky after a while, so I cut it back in early summer, repot it into a nourishing compost, and stand it in our frameyard under some ash trees until it has regained something approaching its natural luxuriance.

— *Good for foliage* —

Foliage plants that I regularly use in pots are the succulent *Cotyledon obtusum*, with loose rosettes of thick, glaucous leaves, and the hare's-foot fern, *Davallia mariesii*, which is deciduous; I also have the evergreen *D. fijeenis*.

On the other side of the house is the terrace where we sit for drinks before lunch. While this catches all the strongest gales, it is wonderfully sheltered from northeasterlies. In May to June I give it over to oxeye daisies, which sow themselves between the paving cracks, but all visible remains of these are removed in late June and are replaced by four large pots with mixed contents that vary a little from year to year, but continue to look pleasing for the next three months.

To break the pot-edge lines, there are ivy-leaved "geraniums" (properly *Pelargoniums*), the double orange nasturtium, *Tropaeolum* 'Hermine Grashoff', blue *Convolvulus saba-*tius (syn. *C. mauritanicus*), and the lax but shrubby *Mimulus glutinosus*, which is apricot-orange, or its variety *M.g. puniceus*, which is coppery. For bushier plants in the center, I rather enjoy the old "geranium" 'A Happy Thought', whose leaves have a yellow central zone while the flowers are cherry-red.

In the Sunk Garden, there are four pots on the piers either side of two stone seats. Their contents vary, but always include the gray-leaved *Helichrysum petiolare*, which has a nice spready habit and tends to twist when the wind is strong rather than break. Some bright orange or red "geraniums" give me the strong color that I feel is needed here. On the floor of the Sunk Garden is a largish pot in whose center I habitually grow one plant of *H. petiolare*, from which I train one branch vertically up a 4ft (1.2m) cane, from which it branches horizontally, like a small conifer. With it, the blue daisies of *Felicia amelloides* and the orange tubular flowers of *Cuphea cyanea* look good. Sometimes, I include an orange mimulus in the arrangement, too.

There's a stone sink in the Sunk Garden in which the brilliant red flowers of *Verbena peruviana* look wonderfully vital. That combines well with the prostrate blue *Lobelia richardsonii*, which is like the cascade types we grow in hanging baskets but is easily perpetuated from cuttings.

My other stone sink is larger. I still like ephemeral, rather than alpine, plants in it for a summer display, though a few of them, notably the pink-flowered *Diascia* 'Ruby Field', overwinter successfully. That goes very well with the prostrate lavender-mauve *Verbena tenuisecta*, but there are all sorts of possibilities, nature sometimes taking a hand, as when self-sown *Cotula coronopifolia*, with yellow buttons, appeared, as also the annual *Calceolaria mexicana*, whose pouched flowers are citrine yellow. I was delighted. Absolute control can become a bore.

CREATING
Displays in pots

Given a backup area, which I have, plants grown in containers (like many bulbs) can be of a kind that make only a brief display of a couple of weeks or so and are then removed to complete their growth cycle in private, or, like the potful shown here, may be of continuing beauty for up to three or four months. Deadheading and feeding the plants may well be their only requirements. With the tubular, orange-flowered *Cuphea cyanea* and the blue daisy, *Felicia amelloides* 'Santa Anita', I grow just one plant of the normally trailing, gray-leaved *Helichrysum petiolare*. I trained one shoot, vertically, up a cane so that it has formed a little tree.

Head start
In my part of the world, Cuphea cyanea *(above) is just about hardy, but it is quicker off the mark from cuttings taken in autumn, overwintered under frost-free glass, and planted out in late spring. Felicia* 'Santa Anita' *is less hardy and is given the same treatment.*

Pulling the scene together
The four pots that stand, in summer, on piers either side of the Sunk Garden pool, make their presence felt when I include in each a vivid red "geranium," as in one of the pots (left). By contrast, the quiet dignity of the background grass's upright habit draws the eye from June, when it flowers, to March, when I finally cut it down. It is Calamagrostis × acutiflora *'Karl Foerster'.*

You never can tell
The official contents of this large, stone sink (below left) include the blue Scaevola aemula, *pink* Diascia *'Ruby Field' and the cream-splashed foliage of variegated* Felicia amelloides. *However, I gained some unexpected additions.* Cotula coronopifolia, *which will also grow floating in water, has seeded itself and has yellow buttons. There are also self-sown seedlings of the acid-yellow annual* Calceolaria mexicana, *which took over completely in the autumn.*

Blues are impossible
As every flower photographer knows, blue has a horrible habit of coming out mauve in reproduction. The trailing blue Lobelia richardsonii *is planted here, in a smallish stone sink (below), with the prostrate* Verbena peruviana, *which has dazzling red flowers. It is the progenitor of many good bedding hybrids. Sometimes, in my climate, it survives the winter, but I would never take a chance on this. Happily to say, though, autumn-struck cuttings root easily.*

AUTUMN

The light in autumn is softer, kinder than in any other season, the year suspended in happy reverie. I love this gentle winding down and surround myself with late flowers – hydrangeas, fuchsias, chrysanthemums. They mingle with seedheads, berries, the coloring foliage of dogwood, Cornus alba, soon to fall and reveal its carmine winter stems.

Autumn highlights

THERE IS NO denying that flower power in my garden (and probably in yours) falls off after the middle of August. A vast concentration of dahlias, cannas, and other tender perennials would be necessary if that were to be prevented. But I love autumn as much as any season, so I instinctively make sure that my garden is still as good as it can be, then. The light at midday is softer and the mellowness of decay can be most relaxing, provided you keep on top of obvious sleaziness. Deadheading, weeding, and watering must continue until late October.

—— Shrubs for color ——

A good many autumn flowers and features are brought into other chapters: bamboos, grasses, bedding, hydrangeas, Michaelmas daisies, ornamental pots, the meadows' second little season. And many autumn flowers are a continuation, as with Japanese anemones, of displays that started in high summer. I should be able to say that of fuchsias, but must confess that my fuchsias' flowering tends to be half-hearted until September. I know that this is in part because of capsid bugs, which feed on the fuchsias' young extension growth, thereby destroying embryo buds and distorting their foliage. But I don't believe that that is the whole story. My red and white

'Mme Cornelissen', for instance, really seems to enjoy the cooler, shorter days of autumn most of all.

The hedging *Fuchsia magellanica* 'Riccartonii' starts to flower a little in June or even earlier, if it has brought its old wood through the winter, but for a gorgeous blood-red display I generally have to wait till September. A colony on the meadow side of the Long Border has a plant of the indigo-blue *Clematis* × *eriostemon* running through a part of it, and they look terrific together, but most of the effort comes from the clematis in June, July, and part of August, at which stage the fuchsia at last joins in wholeheartedly.

Plumbago blue contrasts well with any predominantly red fuchsia, and there are two hardy representatives, both of which I grow. *Ceratostigma plumbaginoides* is a dark blue ground-covering plant whose foliage turns red before dying. If I had the space, I should plant a considerable area of that with intermittent fuchsias, singly or in small groups, rising from among it, while for a winter and spring display, after these two had been cut to the ground, snowdrops, miniature narcissus, crocuses, and scillas.

Ceratostigma willmottianum is more of a shrub, but grows only to 2ft (60cm) in an open border situation. Its heads of disk flowers are a brighter, cleaner blue, but do not appear before

Staying power
The shrubby Salvia microphylla neurepia *(above) is here photographed in autumn. It actually starts up in May and never pauses for the next five months. It is not altogether hardy so it is wise to take a few cuttings each autumn.*

Spring in autumn
Colchicums (right) bring the freshness of spring into autumn. This group is seen in front of the tree mallow, Lavatera olbia, *which has been flowering since early July. It needs cutting away to allow the colchicums some space to flower.*

A succession

The colchicum (above) is an exceedingly generous plant, and can quickly be increased by division of its corms. Here they are interspersed with Stachys coccinea, *a little-known perennial that carries a long succession of coral-red flower spikes. As this is a tender plant, it is treated as an annual, so you must save its seeds. In May, before the colchicum makes its appearance, the area is full of oriental poppies, which are cut right down after flowering.*

Not at all autumnal

The South African hybrid bulb, Nerine x bowdenii (left), has *flowers in brightest pink, which is not an autumnal color, though it flowers in September/October. However deep you plant them, the bulbs will rise to and above the soil surface, but they are surprisingly hardy and will always flower freely, unlike the related* Amaryllis belladonna. Aster amellus *'Violet Queen' grows around and among the nerine.*

September, unless the previous winter was mild. In that case, flowering will start a month earlier, on the old wood.

The shrubby *Salvia microphylla neurepia* has a wonderfully extended season, starting in May (again, if it brought its old wood through the winter intact), but reaching a peak in autumn. Its flowers are a warm rosy red. You might plant it in a sheltered spot with *Eupatorium ligustrinum*, another small, semihardy shrub growing to 3 ft (90cm) with glossy leaves and a succession, from August to November, of rather fluffy, white flower heads. The nearly hardy perennial *Salvia uliginosa* is a boon in the autumn garden. At a time when blue is a rare color, this sage carries short spikes of purest azure flowers, with a white fleck in the center of each. It flowers from mid-August into late

Torchbearer
Red-hot poker can be an inappropriate name for Kniphofia, *in varieties that are white, yellow, or coral. William Robinson called them torch lilies, which is a great improvement. This variety (right) is 'Torchbearer'. Its rather short season arrives in October.*

Not a crocus
The bright chrome-yellow Sternbergia lutea *(left) is a Mediterranean bulb that rests throughout the summer but resurrects itself in October. It needs the hottest position and lightest soil you can provide, in order to flower freely.*

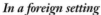

In a foreign setting
Colchicums have no leaves at the time of their autumn flowering. Here I have provided some by bedding out Helichrysum petiolare *'Variegatum' (above) between the corms of* Colchicum speciosum *'Album'. That was in June, after the colchicum's own leaves had withered.*

Youth and old age
Like its prototype, Clematis tangutica, *the larger-flowered 'Bill Mackenzie' (right) carries its single yellow lantern-shaped flowers from June until November. It is perfectly hardy, and I have it over an old espalier pear, which it is slowly killing. Everything has its price.*

autumn and is 6ft (1.8m) tall, needing some support at half that height, but it is a see-through plant so I have it right at the front of the Long Border and I have planted *Lobelia* 'Compliment Scarlet' by its side. These hardy herbaceous lobelias have come on a lot recently. A recent arrival in my garden is 'Tania', a 3ft (90cm) tall lobelia carrying spikes of rich reddish purple flowers.

Gaura lindheimeri would be an excellent foil to these lobelias' strong spikes, itself recalling a swarm of lightly hovering white insects. Our summers are not quite hot enough to make a great success of it in every year, but if you can bring established plants through the winter, they will put on a great display from August on. It is easily raised from seed but late-summer cuttings will get plants started more strongly.

Moisture and a not-too-blazing position suit *Geranium wallichianum* 'Buxton's Variety', one of the best of all the hardy perennial cranesbills. It has a rambling habit and its saucers of blue flowers, white at the center and with dark, purple anthers, appear from July; they are generally a poor shade of mauve early on, the color becoming steadily bluer, however, as the weather begins to cool off.

— *Smaller subjects* —

For a border's margin, a patch of the flower-of-the-west-wind, *Zephyranthes candida*, is most satisfactory after a hot summer, carrying an increasing wealth of white, crocuslike flowers at 6in (15cm) above dark green, rush leaves. Crocus-like flowers are plentiful in autumn. *Sternbergia lutea* is bright chrome-yellow, flowering earlier and more freely on lighter soils than mine. I have this in front of the light purple *Serratula seoanei* (pronounced shawnii), a 2ft (60cm) perennial of twiggy, branching habit, dark foliage and a host of small, thistle flower heads. In winter, it is almost as pretty when its persistent bracts and stamens open to form pale brown rosettes.

Another good partner for that is *Schizostylis coccinea* 'Viscountess Byng', which belongs to a South African group of gladiolus-related perennials with a running rootstock. The spikes of pink flowers are borne rather late in this clone, at their best in November. But the rich red 'Major' comes on in September and often continues for three months. I also have pale pink 'Pallida', salmon pink 'Sunset', and 'Alba', with small white stars. They love moisture, so thrive in heavy soil.

—— *Colchicum combinations* ——
Patches of colchicums (often misnamed autumn crocus) make fine displays in my borders and I don't make a fuss about their foliage in the spring. This is broad, glossy, cabbagey, if you like, but prosperous looking. I like it a lot in April. True, it dies off rather obtrusively in early summer, but it can be cut away as soon as it is brown rather than green. In the runup to that moment, just look at something else. When they flower in autumn, colchicums are without any foliage. You can provide a setting by planting between their clumps, as soon as their foliage has been removed, with some low, rambling foliage plant. Between my *Colchicum speciosum* 'Album' I usually insert pot-grown *Helichrysum petiolare* 'Variegatum', with small heart-shaped leaves. To one side, present the year round, is *Artemisia canescens*, with finely divided gray leaves. Around another patch of colchicums (and there were also oriental poppies, cut back, here), I planted, at midsummer, *Stachys coccinea*, which carried a continuous succession of coral-red flower spikes.

Liriope muscari, with indigo spikes not unlike a grape hyacinth's, is autumn flowering and I have a colchicum called 'The Giant' in front of that. The position is a little too sunny for the liriope, which tends to bleach.

A delightful species
In many ways the species Michaelmas daisies (right) are healthier and more elegant than the man-made hybrids. This is Aster turbinellus. *In front, grow* Fuchsia magellanica *'Versicolor'.*

———— • ————

Rewarding
This smoky bush (left), now designated Cotinus coggygria *'Rubrifolius group', has charming foliage, though not of the deepest coloring. It is joined, in early July, by a haze of purplish 'smoke'.*

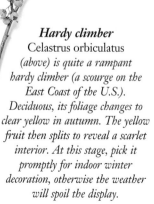

Hardy climber
Celastrus orbiculatus (above) is quite a rampant hardy climber (a scourge on the East Coast of the U.S.). Deciduous, its foliage changes to clear yellow in autumn. The yellow fruit then splits to reveal a scarlet interior. At this stage, pick it promptly for indoor winter decoration, otherwise the weather will spoil the display.

Good, hardy fuchsia
*Fuchsia 'Genii' (left) gives best
results if treated as a herbaceous
plant, cutting it to the ground in the
New Year, at which season
interplanted snowdrops will make
their display. The fuchsia's lime-green
foliage (each leaf and young stem is
red) keeps on getting better through
the summer, and is finally joined by
a generous display of red
and purple blossom.*

Among yet another group of colchicums, in the Wall Garden, I have planted the snowdrop, *Galanthus nivalis* 'Samuel Arnott', so they do turn and turn about. And the last planting with which I shall bother you, in the same garden, is in front of *Lavatera olbia*, the tree mallow. They are almost exactly the same color. Harmony at last! I have to cut the mallow back in early September, to give the colchicums breathing space.

When my colchicums have multiplied and become overcrowded in the borders, I transfer surplus stock to the meadow areas, and it is the same with crocuses. But I have not yet ventured to move *Crocus pulchellus*, an October performer with pale mauve flowers, out into turf because it looks so fragile. But it has increased well, so I must try. That grows on the shady side of the Barn Garden with *Saxifraga fortunei*, a late-flowering, herbaceous species having rounded, scalloped leaves, and a foam of intriguingly lopsided white flowers, in which the lowest two petals are much longer than the rest.

— *Striking effects* —

I grow several of the latest-flowering red-hot pokers together. 'Torchbearer' is a good, straight yellow, 5ft (1.4m) tall, while *Kniphofia rooperi*, at 4ft (1.2m), is orange and has short cones, notably broad at the base. It looks good in the same eyeful as the white brushes of the pampas, *Cortaderia selloana* 'Pumila', but the kniphofia flowers only for ten days or so.

Some of the late aconites (or monkshoods), notably the forms of *Aconitum carmichaelii*, deep blue or indigo, are good

foils for lighter colors, like the white *Cimicifugas*. We always knew this species as *Aconitum fischeri* and it was in the Wall Garden from the first. It is already showing its young foliage in January but does not flower until October, by which time its leaves are changing to yellow.

Most of my periwinkles are spring-flowering – we have a long bank of the white form of *Vinca minor* in a hot, dry position at the foot of a yew hedge and it flowers its head off. Vincas are repeatedly recommended for shade but flower ten times more freely in a light position.

So it is with *V. difformis* but the principal flowering season in this periwinkle is autumn. The flowers look as though they had been given a slanting cut on one side of each petal, like a propeller. They are pale mauve. If the winter was mild, they will build up, in the next spring, to another generous flowering in May, but this is not quite as hardy as other periwinkles.

— *Shrubs for autumn* —

A couple of autumn-flowering shrubs must be brought in. I have two 10ft (3m) specimens of *Ligustrum quihoui*, a September-flowering privet, almost deciduous, with small narrow leaves and cascading panicles of white blossom in the greatest profusion. Of course, it has the usual privet smell; if you like the plant enough, you can learn to like its scent. I have become perfectly tolerant of privets.

Escallonia bifida is none too hardy, alas; neither is it easily struck from cuttings. But it is an extremely fast and vigorous grower. For six weeks from early September, it is covered with domed panicles of pure white stars and these, on every suitable occasion, are covered with eagerly supping butterflies.

I mentioned the hawthorn, *Crataegus persimilis* 'Prunifolia', at the time of its flowering in my Spring Flowers chapter (see pages 10-17). That will now be laden with dark red haws until set upon after leaf fall, from the top of the tree downward, by mistle thrushes. The leaves themselves usually take on glowing colors on some of the branches, the remainder falling a rather wan yellow. Best for its fruit is *C. laciniata*, by the front path. Its gray cut leaves are always charming and the clusters of white blossom are an added bonus in June. But in early October, when the large haws change to a luminous, light-orange color, they are a spectacle.

The advantages of walls

RETAINING WALLS, generally uncemented, are built to hold back soil in such a way as to take up any changes in level by a series of verticals and horizontals rather than in the natural progression of a bank. Step-risers are themselves retaining walls. They, and the larger walls, are a great home for many plants. The soil behind a wall is cool and moist, yet drainage is excellent.

— *Good subjects for walls* —

Gardening architects love retaining walls and Lutyens at Dixter went to town with them in a series of terraces, since the garden lies on a southwest facing slope. Then, when my father created the Sunk Garden, after the First World War, 3ft (90cm) high sandstone retaining walls were built all around that. They were planted with choice alpines, and some of the heavy, engraved metal labels are still there. Even a few of the plants remain: encrusted saxifrages like *Saxifraga marginata*, and the cobweb houseleek, *Sempervivum arachnoideum*.

Gardening with alpines is not in my line, however. The garden is too big, and there isn't time to give them the attention they deserve. But there are plenty of pretty plants to colonize these walls without requiring any attention. Aubrieta is one of the best. It makes great pendulous cushions and will even tolerate a north aspect, if required to.

Its natural color is a straightforward mauve and because it self-sows, it tends to revert to this from the more glamorous pinks and purples, but there is variation enough. It is at its best on the lower terrace, just above the dry moat, and along the back drive (down to the kitchen yard).

A charming, unpremeditated feature, here are the primroses, some plain, some colored, that have seeded themselves among the aubrietas. Another welcome interloper is *Euphorbia amygdaloides* var. *robbiae*. Normally you expect to see this spurge in shade, whether dry or moist, but when a plant self-sows you may learn that it has quite different ideas from those we ascribe to it. In its kitchen-drive site it is in full sun. Its lime-green flowers appear in spring, as usual, but, under the influence of the sun's heat, take on a glowing coral red in July, as they are fading. That never happens in shade.

Other walls are mainly colonized by the little Mexican daisy, *Erigeron karvinskianus*, which is a wonderful do-it-yourself plant. Its season starts in May, when the young flowers are white, but continues right into early winter.

As each flower ages, its rays change to pink, so the plants acquire a parti-coloring. It is just as happy in paving cracks. Eventually, all the flowered growth

Early-flowering team
I like Bergenia stracheyi *(above) for its neat foliage, reliability of flowering and clear coloring. At its best in March, it just overlaps the long season of* Euphorbia amygdaloides *var.* robbiae.

———•———

For sun or shade
Euphorbia amygdaloides *var.* robbiae *(left) is usually recommended for shade. But in several parts of my garden, it has seeded itself into sunny steps and walls. Not only is it perfectly happy here, but as the inflorescences are going over they change in sunshine to soft red tints.*

Great pads of mauve
This aubrieta wall (right), which
supports the lower terrace, makes a
fine background in April to the
tapestry of naturalized and wild
flowers in the drained upper moat.

Back drive view
The retaining walls (below) are
heavily colonized by aubrietas, ferns,
spurges and primroses. The topiary
peacocks are still at their smartest, not
yet having come into new growth.
Sorry we haven't caught up with the
weeding yet, but that follows
in due course.

gives the plant a shabby look. Some time in late winter or early spring, we cut them all back as hard as we can. Any that are encroaching on precious things, I pull out.

Among the plants that have escaped from their border sites and into walls or step-risers, is *Omphalodes cappadocica*, which is especially good in shade, its rich blue forget-me-not flowers having a long, spring season. *Erinus alpinus* is good in shade (as well as sun) and the white-flowered variant shows up best, there. Ferns, of course, are excellent. They have a section in this book to themselves on pages 106-11.

Once a wall has been built, it is not too easy to plant into it. One way to overcome this difficulty is by planting at the top or at its foot and to hope that your protégée will seed itself into the cracks, or else, if such is its habit, run about in them. *Campanula portenschlagiana* and *C. poscharskyana* will do this. Planted at the foot of a wall, the latter also will climb.

From being planted at the top, *Geranium dalmaticum*, with rosy lilac flowers in early summer on quite a dense cushion,

will also thread its way through the cracks at a lower level. So will the wild toadflax, with 2ft (60cm) tall spikes of yellow flowers, but that is too invasive in most situations.

I love to see red valerian, *Centranthus ruber*, in walls and paving, but it is a muscular perennial, and its thick roots can be horribly disruptive to the fabric of a wall, so I allow it only in moderation. The red-flowered and the white are the most effective, rather than the deep pink, which is rather muddy. After its first flowering, about the turn of June/July, we cut the plants as hard back as they'll go. This not only stops them seeding too freely, but encourages a second flush of bloom.

We don't have wallflowers actually in our walls (though we could well have) but they are in the step-risers at the north-west end of the house and here they indefinitely maintain their colony by self-sowing. The flowers are small, often striped yellow, showing virus infection, but they smell delicious, and they have an air of freedom, varying greatly in height according to their age, which bedded plants do not.

Mexican (takeover) daisy
This little daisy, Erigeron karvinskianus (syn. mucronatus) sows itself (below) into walls and steps of every aspect, although it is happiest in sunshine. It flowers nonstop from May to November.

Well-drained perch
Tree lupines, Lupinus arboreus (right), love free drainage and often perch themselves, from self-sown seed, on wall tops. They never live more than three years but fresh supplies are always handy.

Two of the most surprising wall occupants on the Sunk Garden walls are self-sown *Paeonia delavayi*, a 'tree' peony with maroon flowers in May, and a red hot poker, *Kniphofia*. I hoped and tried to establish the glaucous-leaved and somewhat woody *K. caulescens* in a similar position, but failed.

One of my signal successes, however, has been a *Juniperus sabina tamariscifolia*, which I planted many years ago on top of the Sunk Garden wall. After cascading down the face of the wall, this juniper has spread out like an apron over the floor 3ft (90cm) lower down.

Besides the house itself, there are a number of old farm buildings at Dixter that Lutyens incorporated into his garden design, and there are certain free-standing walls, though not nearly as many as

Beautiful thug
Red valerian, Centranthus ruber (opposite), also shown with Erigeron karvinskianus (left), is the particular bête noire of architects who have the care of old walls and ruins. The long thick roots are notoriously destructive. But their beauty is irresistible. I swiftly cut them back after their first May–June flowering, in red, two shades of pink, and white, and am rewarded with a second crop of flowers in September.

Lutyens would have liked, since my father preferred yew hedges, so much cheaper to install if not to maintain. The plants that I grow to take advantage of these walls can be divided into three categories: fruit, climbers, and wall shrubs.

— *My favorite fruit* —

Figs are the most striking fruits trained to the walls at Great Dixter in two places: the weather-boarded barn on the northeast side of the Barn Garden and the brick wall between the upper and lower terraces on the southwest side of the house. These figs were planted for their ornamental foliage and so 'Brunswick', with plentifully lobed leaves, was chosen.

I adore green figs and am the archetypal fig pig. Every three or four years, 'Brunswick' ripens a crop that is worth protecting. The fruits are the largest of any variety cultivated in this country, and a seductive shade of brown with longitudinal splits when fully ripe. It is quite a business securing them from other contestants, especially birds and wasps. When, from mid-August to late September, I see that a fruit is just beginning to change from uniform green, I enclose it in a perforated lettuce bag and secure this with a twist-it tie to the supporting branch behind. In good weather, the fruit will be dead ripe in three days' time. The bag (and fruit) is removed and re-used on the next ripening fruit.

In many years, the putative fruits, then not much larger than a pea and fully exposed near the tips of last year's shoots (the leaves not yet expanded), are reduced to pulp by an April frost. The less you prune a fig the greater its potential for fruiting, but because the trees have to be kept close to their walls, we have a go at them every third year.

129

The apricot, growing against the warmer face of the house, is as old as the garden. It flowers regularly, a web of white blossom each March, but bears a good crop only every third year or so. The flavor is unbelievably good compared to that of imported fruit. There are peaches too, but they seldom live for longer than 40 years, and a few Morello cherries on north-facing walls. Even when the fruit is netted, the blackbirds nearly always get the better of us there.

Then there are the pears. I do nothing for them, except tie them in when necessary and each winter prune all young growth back to heavy old spurs. Some of them act as frames for clematis and other climbers. And I love their blossom, with its sickly sweet scent.

— Useful climbers —

Of the self-clinging climbers, my favorite ivy, of which I have two large specimens, is *Hedera colchica* 'Dentata Variegata'. It is the only one I know whose leaves, when crushed, have a

sweet and pleasant fragrance (of gin). They are large and luminous with their bold cream variegation.

The one on a shady wall in the Wall Garden has *Clerodendrum bungei* growing (from its own suckers) immediately in front of it and they make a handsome couple. The clerodendrum has large, dark green heart-leaves and terminal heads of deep pink, sweetly scented blossom in autumn.

Hedera helix 'Buttercup' is another good climber on the Hovel alongside the Topiary Garden. This yellow-leaved ivy needs to receive enough light, otherwise it becomes green, yet in too blazing a position it will scorch. Here, not receiving sunlight till the afternoon and then only in the summer, it is perfectly suited. It makes a good background to yellow mulleins, or to white *Nicotiana sylvestris* or the white sweet rocket (*Hesperis*) when I grow these favorites in the border in front.

There are three self-clinging climbers in the hydrangea family that I like to grow. They are all white-flowered. First in bloom is *Hydrangea anomala* (*H. petiolaris*), in June. This plant

Traditional north-waller
The sour but most excellently flavored Morello cherry (above) is one of the most satisfactory of north-wall inhabitants. Its blossom is purest white.

Fine tapestry
The autumn-flowering Clerodendrum bungei *(right) placed itself against a north wall, bang in front of a variegated ivy. The resulting tapestry is most satisfactory.*

fully deserves its popularity, although it has to be admitted that its display of lacecaps lasts for only three weeks at the outside. But its foliage changes to a luminous shade of yellow in October, which looks all the better if you site the plant against a sunny wall, though it is also happy in full shade.

Schizophragma integrifolium outside my kitchen window, flowers next, in July. The handsome lacecap bracts on this plant are diamond shaped and much larger and more striking than the hydrangea's, but young plants are slow to mature. I think mine was eight or nine years old before it flowered. Then, again, the young spring shoots are extremely susceptible to late frost damage. One way or another, there are quite a few non-flowering years. But it's a winner when it performs. The sacrifice of waiting for its big moment is not felt too greatly in a large garden like Dixter where there's so much else of value to divert one's attention.

Pileostegia viburnoides is the last of this trio in flower, melting into a froth of creamy white in September. Furthermore, its foliage is evergreen and distinctly handsome. Give it lots of food and drink and it will do you proud. Mine, in the Wall Garden, has a hortensia hydrangea in front of it.

— *Sinuous charmers* —

Of the twining or tendril-clinging climbers, the biggest is *Wisteria sinensis*. I have the same widely distributed clone that was originally imported from China early in the nineteenth century and always vegetatively propagated since then. It is eminently satisfactory, flowering abundantly each May,

whether I've pruned it or not, and yielding a small but welcome crop in late summer. Its warm scent epitomizes summer to me. Sometimes sparrows take to stripping its flower buds in late winter. A few strands of black cotton stretched between the branch tips puts a stop to this. Much of my plant festoons the huge *Magnolia × soulangeana* 'Lennei', so I have to prune the wisteria fairly heavily to keep it in order.

Nearby, on the same terrace wall, is the white summer jasmine, *Jasminum officinale* 'Affine' which is the most vigorous strain. That flowers from early July and drenches the terrace with scent at night and in the early morning. It is well worth leaving the terrace door into the house open for this, as well as for the myrtle in August. A good partner with the jasmine, being of equal vigor so that neither could kill the other, was the white *Clematis montana*. Its curtain of blossom was a sight in May and its vanilla scent very powerful. But it had been weakening over the last few years (it was nearly 80 years old, after all) and, for a change, I have replaced it with the deep pink montana, 'Freda'. I hope it can cope.

I have, of course, many other clematis scattered about the garden, not so much on walls as growing over other shrubs or as vertical features up poles. There are two interesting climbers on the barn and oast walls in the Barn Garden. *Solanum jasminoides* 'Album' has as warm a nook as any in the garden. If winters are kind, it flowers prodigiously from late June to early December, with much showier jasmine-like blossom than jasmine itself, but no sweet scent. If it doesn't bring its old growth through the winter, it gets going so late the next

Outside my kitchen
On a northeast aspect, Hedera colchica 'Dentata Variegata' (right), whose foliage, when crushed, is sweetly scented, has taken charge of most of my kitchen wall. When it reaches beyond the gutter, I have to take stern action. I can just see through Schizophragma integrifolium, almost obliterating daylight from my stove, to the purple phloxes beyond.

131

summer that it hardly flowers at all, and it pays to have a young plant in reserve in the greenhouse ready to plant out in the spring. That soon takes off.

Schisandra rubriflora is nearby but in shade for most of the day. Its flower buds are like cherry stones; they open to small, waxy red lanterns. I have a male and a female plant, and the latter, given a pollinator, carries tassels of red berries in September, far more showy than its flowers. Unfortunately my lady, for unexplained reasons, has been dying back over the last few years and I have planted another. It is, I am pleased to note, a perfectly hardy plant.

— *Wall shrubs* —

It is usually for added warmth and protection that shrubs are planted close to, or actually trained against, walls, but in some cases this is a good place for a perfectly hardy shrub with a lax habit, since this can be countered by securing it to the wall here and there. Such is the case of the *Magnolia × soulangeana* 'Lennei', the magnolia mentioned as a host for my wisteria. It has deep pink goblets over a long April-May season, so it overlaps with the wisteria. Beneath it is a carpet of pale blue *Scilla bithynica*, which extends this area's season by flowering in March, when the magnolia's branches are still bare. By the time the scilla is in leafy gloom, it is resting for the summer.

The winter-flowering jasmine, *Jasminum nudiflorum,* is another lax shrub that benefits from wall support; you clip it hard back after flowering. Its yellow blossom is immensely cheering. But the nearby *Abutilon megapotamicum* needs every available scrap of warmth and sunshine, although it is never actually killed by cold. Like the solanum, it will flower from June to midwinter if it manages to bring its old growth through the previous winter. Its tri-colored lanterns are in red, yellow, and brown.

Some clematis, especially the evergreens, flower much more freely if grown against a warm wall. *Clematis armandii* is the best known and I have the clone that purports to be 'Snowdrift', though it is unlike the 'Snowdrift' I knew 40 years ago and has the disadvantage of very long internodes, which makes for a rangy habit.

A recent acquisition and a great success is the evergreen species, *C. finetiana*, from China. Its foliage is smaller and more elegant than in *C. armandii*. Its growth is abundant and is smothered in July with great swags of small white blossoms. Their greatest asset, perhaps, is the tremendous fragrance that they impart for a considerable distance all around them. The comparison with eau-de-Cologne is not far off the mark. This clematis is growing against the house over an espalier pear where there is a southwest aspect so I don't yet really know how exposed a position it would tolerate.

On the hottest house wall, facing southeast and sheltered from cold winds, there is a pomegranate, *Punica granatum*, a present from our cousins when they lived at Standen in West Sussex in the 1930s. That has a scattering of brilliant scarlet flowers (not large, though) in summer, but it has only twice set

Lightning deflector
Above, is an ancient house leek (older than me, anyway), which is said to protect your house from being struck by lightning. (I shouldn't depend on it.)

Developing apricots
Choisya ternata (above) is the obvious May feature against this southwest wall, but the ancient apricot behind it is of greater importance to me. Crops are erratic but luscious.

None-too-hardy
The common myrtle, Myrtus communis (far left), has as warm a wall as we can give it, on the upper terrace. The fragrance of its August blossom wafts right through the house, when the terrace door is propped open. Its purplish-black fruits ripen only after hot summers. Hebe 'Jewel' is in my Long Border. It flowers on and off (deadheading promotes the next flush) from early summer to Christmas and is sweetly scented.

Dazzling blue
Ceanothus flowers rarely come out as blue as they should in photographs. This evergreen May-flowerer is 'Puget Blue', growing against a warm, southeast wall (left). It has plenty of space, so I don't need to prune it.

fruit and never ripened any. Next to it I have, until I get tired of it, *Buddleia salviifolia*, a native of South Africa, but which I saw making magnificent spring-flowering tree specimens when I was on a visit to Victoria, Australia. Its leaves are sagelike, but scarred and battered by winter's end. Thus it offers no fit setting for the lavender blossom in May. Next to that is the evergreen *Ceanothus* 'Puget Blue', with a powerfully dense display of blossom in May to June.

The other somewhat tender buddleia that I grow, this one next to the magnolia I have just described, is *Buddleia auriculata*. It has panicles of demure, buff-colored blossom, but in October to November, and is marvelously scented. Like the abutilon, it sometimes gets cut to the ground by a hard winter, but it can perpetuate itself from root cuttings and so, once it is well established, you'll never lose it.

— *Good performers* —

Close by is *Azara microphylla*, which can make a small evergreen tree, winters permitting. Its neat, gleaming, boxlike foliage is pleasing. It flowers in early spring: a powder of tiny yellow wisps on the branch undersides, totally insignificant were it not for the great gusts of chocolatey scent that it gives off. The origin of that has puzzled many visitors. I also grow *A. serrata*, which makes an almost embarrassingly large shrub, winters permitting. That has quite sizable leaves and conspicuous pouffes of yellow stamens in May, with a delicious fresh-fruit-salad fragrance. My original plant became so scarred and unwieldy that I replaced it with a youngster. Cuttings normally strike readily.

Although it could get killed at any moment, I am currently immensely proud of one of the Californian tree poppies, *Dendromecon harfordii* (as it is identified by Californian friends, though generally misidentified in England as the inferior *D. rigida*). Above tough, glaucous, lance-shaped leaves (most unpoppylike), it carries pure yellow poppy flowers all summer, but most freely in May, when they are open in the mornings, closing after lunch. *Dendromecon harfordii* is one of those precious plants of which I am careful to keep a reserve of a few rooted cuttings in case of accidents.

My favorite wall shrub is the common Mediterranean myrtle, *Myrtus communis*, which, as I said, grows close to the garden door leading on to our terrace. It has a wonderful spicy scent on the air. In good years, flowering is followed by a crop of handsome purple fruits, which ripen in November.

— *For cool walls* —

Piptanthus nepalensis is useful on a shady wall, though it is as happy in sun. Fastgrowing, its bold, trifoliate leaves are almost evergreen. The trusses of substantial yellow pea flowers open in succession for six weeks around May, and they cut well for the house. The down side is that this shrub, in middle age, is liable to an unexplained die-back on a scattering of branches.

Perhaps the best of all northwallers is the despised (but not by me, because so common and easily grown,) *Cotoneaster horizontalis*. It will hoist itself up a wall face without assistance and the fishbone structure of its layered branches is always interesting. Thanks to the birds spreading its berries around, you'll see a lot of this particular shrub in various parts of the garden, even though I often have to be firm with misplaced seedlings, removing any that are in the wrong place.

Ornamental grasses

I LOVE THE ornamental grasses but have strong views on how they should, and should not, be used. Their thin strap leaves are in telling contrast to most other foliage we use and, indeed, to any architectural features in a garden. What's more, the airy, fountainlike habit of many grasses (by no means all, nor all the time, for they can radically change in character between the beginning and the end of a growing season) often suggests that they should stand well clear of the plants around them; otherwise their personality is smothered. There is no surer way of smothering it than by herding all your grasses together, so that the eye becomes confused with so much similarity. Yet, for lack of ideas on how best to use them, many public, botanical or societies' gardens do just that. "If you see them all together, you'll best be able to decide which are for you", the argument will run. But compartmentalizing is the enemy of gardening as art.

The largest and most dramatic grass I grow – entirely for its foliage, in this case – is the giant reed grass, *Arundo donax*. In two positions, the Rose Garden and the paved floor of the Sunk Garden, it stands in solitary splendor, like a sculpture, in complete contrast with all about it. Its blue-gray, rather broad leaves could almost have been wrought from metal but, of course, the lightest breeze sets them in motion. Elsewhere, I have two groups, quite close to one another. The first is right on the edge of a path. As the plant rises to 10 to 13 ft (3 to 4m) in the course of one growing season, this might seem a trifle odd. There is a considerable planting of hydrangeas behind it, and my second group of *Arundo donax*, more conventionally, is sited in the middle of them.

— *Graceful fountains* —

My next tallest grass, at 10 ft (3m), is *Miscanthus floridulus*, in the Barn Garden. Again it is a leaves-only species, rarely flowering in our climate. It is like a green fountain, and in front of it I do have another, but entirely different grass, *Stipa splendens*. In this, the leaves are of no account; the inflorescence is the thing. At its flowering, in July, it is fluffed out and green, but closes into fawn-colored tails on ripening, and so remains throughout the autumn and winter.

Rather similar in its behavior is *Calamagrostis* × *acutiflora* 'Karl Foerster', perhaps the most versatile of all grasses. At its early-summer flowering it is all grace, with puffed out, soft purple flower heads on such flexible, 6 ft (1.8 m) stems that any shower, or even a heavy dew, sways them sideways to the

Solitary giant
One of the most handsome grasses is Arundo donax *(above). Although it can make about 10ft (3m) in one growing season, I also use it at the edge of a path. Tallest plants should not necessarily be sited farthest from you. The jungle feel of plunging right past these giant grasses is exciting.*

Soft and fluffy
Calamagrostis × acutiflora *'Karl Foerster' (left), which ends
its life pale and stiff, starts its long season with soft gusts of
purplish blossom. They sway to the ground in rain, but always
right themselves. The mat-forming* Erigeron glaucus
is flowering in front.

Engulfed in blossom
Here is Helictotrichon sempervirens *(above) during its May-June
flowering, when it is engulfed in campanulas, foxgloves and double
white dianthus. This evergreen, perennial grass is
normally seen as a stiff and sedate porcupine
cushion of glaucous foliage.*

135

Fall scene
*Perhaps this October picture
(right) explains why I am so fond of
my garden in autumn. The white
pampas plumes belong to* Cortaderia
selloana *'Pumila'.* Spartina
pectinata *and* Hakonechloa
macra *can also be seen.*

— • —

The tall and the short of it
*In closeup (left), the two grasses
photographed in situ (right). The 3ft (1m)
high* Spartina pectinata *'Aureomarginata'
looks like big brother to* Hakonechloa
macra *'Aureola'.*

ground. But they are strong and return to the
vertical as soon as dry. I have one plant on
either side of the Barn Garden. A mat of the
mauve daisy, *Erigeron glaucus*, flowers in July
around the base of the first. The second can be
seen playing the part of sentinel over an autumn
planting of asters and nerines in October. By then, the grass
has bleached to palest fawn in stiff rods, and it remains so till
spring, when at last I cut it down.

The leaves could hardly be less interesting, but who cares?
So it is also with another prima donna, *Stipa gigantea*. That is
ideal to grow on a promontory, as I have it at the bottom of the
Long Border, but I initially made the mistake of planting it
too near the corner where the path makes a right angle. When
in flower, its stems got knocked and broken by passersby.

— Arresting features —

Stipa gigantea expands in June like a peacock displaying, to a
height and breadth of 6ft (1.8m). Its oatlike flowerheads, rose-
tinted at first, later bleaching to parchment, create a diapha-
nous veil through which, in July, you can see the neighboring
campanulas and hydrangeas. In autumn, it forms a background to *Fuchsia* 'Genii'. After that, rough weather wrecks it.
The best you can do is to sort out the dead stuff, wearing
gloves so that you can use them like a comb. I once tried cutting the whole plant back, but it didn't like that at all and
hardly flowered the next season.

With pampas grass, *Cortaderia selloana*, you can do that in
spring. I grow the relatively dwarf 5ft to 6ft (1.2 to 1.8m)
variety, 'Pumila', which carries a dense array of upright
brushes. There are two clumps of that in the Barn Garden and
we have planted quite a colony in the new prairie.

The many varieties of *Miscanthus sinensis* have a fountain
habit, especially 'Gracillimus', with narrow leaves and a pale
median stripe; and 'Variegatus', wherein pale, marginal
stripes give extra lightness. These we grow entirely for their
foliage because with our cool summers they never flower sig-
nificantly. 'Purpurascens' is another such, at 3ft (1m) rather

Tongue-twister
Roll this off your tongue: Molinia *caerulea arundinacea*
'Transparent'. This one (above), like other molinias, flowers in
autumn and makes a striking, yet graceful cornerpiece.

•

Happy couple
Here you see Spartina pectinata *and* Hakonechloa macra *(left), and a pretty pair they make,*
provided I cut down the spartina once a year.

CARING FOR
Grasses

"He writes as the grass grows," said Joseph
Conrad of W. H. Hudson, the field naturalist.
But even grasses need to be treated with
respect. I originally purchased this one, *Stipa
gigantea*, as bare-root plants in autumn, and the
whole lot died. As I later discovered, many
grasses hate to be disturbed just as they are
approaching dormancy. Split and replant them
as much as you like in spring or summer, when
they can immediately resume active growth to
make good their lost roots, but in autumn they
have no such resilience. Neither can you cut
this stipa hard back in spring without losing
most of its subsequent blossom. With pampas
grass, you can do so with impunity.

shorter than the average. Its leaves are purplish when young
and they take on excellent autumn tints. I find it a good foil in
the border for annual flowers as seen in the background here.
'Silver Feather' (correctly 'Silberfeder') is an early example of
a new line of varieties from German breeders that will flower
effectively in northern climates, before winter's arrival. I have
it in the Long Border with a bush of *Pinus mugo* in front, to
hide its legs. Grasses go very well with conifers.

Dwarf grasses are no less endearing. *Helictotrichon semper-*
virens (so harshly served by its name) makes a lowish porcupine of stiff, glaucous foliage above which, in May, its graceful
flowering stems rise to more than 3ft (1m). I use this at the
border margin with some *Geranium sanguineum* 'Shepherd's
Warning' peering out of its skirts, but it is also a strong feature
to grow in paving cracks. One I grow like this is actually a
grass-like sedge, *Carex buchananii*, a soft yet vital brown.
Another is *Molinia caerulea* 'Moorhexe', only 2ft (60cm) tall
and with stiff, knitting-needle stems in autumn.

One of my most graceful grasses, though only 1ft (30cm)
tall, goes by the forbidding name of *Hakonechloa macra*
'Aureola'. Its flexible leaves are variegated in green and
yellow, and it bursts into unexpected blossom in October.
Rising through this, and confusing the onlooker, is
a 3ft (90cm) green-and-yellow variegated
grass, *Spartina pectinata* 'Aureomarginata'.
This is a quite aggressive spreader, so I
frequently check it by wrenching
out every shoot in sight.

Many grasses are
autumn flowering. *Pani-*
cum virgatum, of which I have
the clone 'Haense Herms', is
nothing to look at until it becomes
all specks and spaces in September.

Still game in midwinter
Many flowering grasses hold on to
their inflorescences in a decorative
manner, deep into winter. Storm
winds usually finish them. Meantime,
grass skeletons (above) do much to
furnish my garden, at least
till Christmas.

Perennial asters

PERENNIAL ASTERS, which we know collectively (though often misleadingly) as Michaelmas daisies, were mainstays of our autumn borders some 30 years ago. It was the large-flowered types that were mostly preferred, and to which the breeders gave their attention. These were varieties of *Aster novi-belgii*. But it was these very favorites that then became a burden to grow well, because they fell prey to one crippling pest and several diseases, notably mildew. None of the other aster species or their offspring have suffered in the same way, and because these are anyway much the most graceful and, to me, attractive, I do not feel the loss keenly. The recent aster trials at the Royal Horticultural Society's garden, Wisley, have excluded *A. novi-belgii*, more or less.

I will start with two asters that form the nucleus of a gay autumn planting of which I am rather proud. 'Veilchenkönigin' ('Violet Queen') is quite an old variety of *Aster amellus* and I particularly like it for its upstanding habit (rare in this species), though only 15in (38cm) tall, and for the richness of its blue-purple coloring. The other, 'Andenken an Alma Pötschke', underlines the fact that the Germans have been some of the most successful hybridizers, but that they have little regard for a good-selling name outside the small coterie who knew the lady here celebrated. This is an *A. novae-angliae*

cultivar, characterized by rough, hairy stems and leaves and, given an open site, an upstanding habit combined with immunity from any ailments. Its flowers are a brilliant, almost disconcerting, shade of carmine pink. I have combined these with interplanted *Nerine bowdenii*, a South African amaryllid with heads of equally brilliant and unautumnal pink flowers. The supporting cast is represented by *Artemisia* 'Powis Castle' for gray foliage, and the upright rods of the grass, *Calamagrostis* × *acutiflora* 'Karl Foerster'.

All this is in the Barn Garden where I have two other asters. The species *Aster turbinellus* grows 4ft (1.2m) tall, and needs a strong cane and two ties for each clump within a group. Its stems, prior to flowering, open into a fine, purple-green network. The flowers themselves are purple with a small yellow disk. This is elegant and charming. Then, there is a recent acquisition, *A. pringlei* 'Monte Cassino', with fine, linear leaves and a haze of tiny white flowers. It is about 3ft (90cm) tall and flowers for a long time, being equally successful as a cut flower, for which purpose it is particularly popular in Holland and Germany.

— *Asters with exceptional merits* —

In the Long Border, I have two patches of *Aster sedifolius*, which was in the border (then known as *A. acris*) from its inception. It flowers for a month from mid-August and, at 3ft (90cm), makes a solid platform of interlocked mauve blossom. Spidery as individuals, these are wonderfully voluptuous in the mass. I like to have scarlet nasturtiums threading their way through this, but often they refuse to do as I wish. *A. ericoides* 'Esther', right at the border's front and only 2ft (60cm) tall at most, has exceptional merits. Its fine leaves are the freshest green right through the summer (most Michaelmas daisies are boring in the run-up to flowering). Small, pinky mauve flowers start to appear like stars at dusk, in September, building to a full-throated chorus in mid-October.

Trouble-free
The popular, large-flowered cultivars Aster novi-belgii *have developed at the expense of their resistance to pests and diseases. By contrast, the other species remain of the easiest cultivation.* A. Turbinellus *(far left) has a network of dark stems and leaves throughout the summer, leading up to a delightful autumn display, at 4ft (1.2m), of lavender-blue blossom. The pure white* A. pringlei *'Monte Cassino' (left) which is 3ft (1m) tall, first came to prominence as a cut flower and is even longer lasting on the plant.*

Summer brilliance
The vivid coloring both in Aster amellus *'Violet Queen' and the*
carmine pink A. novae-angliae *'Andenken an Alma Pötschke' (above)*
reigns in autumn yet seems to belong more appropriately to
summer, so I have combined them with the equally dashing
bulb, Nerine × bowdenii.

In the High Garden, I have my last remaining *Aster novi-belgii*, an old variety called 'Climax', with single flowers of good lavender with a prominent yellow disk. It grows to nearly 5 ft (1.4m), and is not self-supporting. I could correct this by pinching out its shoot tips when it is 2 ft (60cm) tall.

In the border opposite are two varieties of *A. cordifolius*. They self-sow freely. The basal heart-shaped leaves are a distinguishing character in this species, though not always visible at flowering. But it is a good sprayer, apt to be a little wishy-washy, perhaps. I should acquire a cultivar of more definite coloring, like the blue 'Little Carlow'.

The species *Aster diffusus* is a pet, utterly prostrate, with small fans of white blossom in the second half of October. I have it on a corner, but its flowering season is short.

You emerge from the High Garden through the yew archway to confront my *pièce de résistance*. This used to be the lavender garden, with double rows of dwarf lavender connecting my father's yew topiary pieces. But lavender hates our heavy soil; plants were always being killed by a miserable disease called shab. Once you have lost a unit in a hedge, you can never make good. So, more than 15 years ago now, I decided to change over to an aster that had always been in the garden, *Aster lateriflorus* 'Horizontalis'. It makes a sturdy plant, often mistaken for a shrub before flowering, 3 ft (90cm) or less tall, and with strong horizontal branching. Leaves and stems are purplish green, and the flowers, which start to open in early September, are small, whitish, but, the rays being laid back, with a prominent purple disk. The tide of blossom increases to a peak in mid-October.

In front is a ribbon of *Persicaria vacciniifolia*, a mat-forming polygonum with upright pokers only a few inches tall and pinky mauve. This is at its best in late summer and autumn but it insists on moisture and thus suffers in drought years. Also it requires a lot of weeding.

Between the double line of asters I have a row of deep blue 'English' irises, *Iris latifolia*, which flower late in June. The rising tide of asters conceals the dying iris leaves. In winter, the aster hedges retain their shape.

WINTER

The wind is easterly, as all three oast house cowls agree, and there is rime on the lawn. Winter can be very beautiful and there are many good shapes in my garden. Most often it is gloomy and vile. But the plants need it and it is by no means dead; a sleep at most, with much visibly going on in the plant world.

The winter scene

TO THE GARDENER, who lives close to the earth, winter is not the long, depressing season that it appears to those divorced from it. True, we not infrequently experience snow at Easter, but then, no less, there can be an abundance of spring flowers with soft winds as early as January.

The worst aspect of winter is in its short days and overcast skies. But the plants are never truly dormant, and even as the snow melts, it is easy to see that daffodils and other bulbs have been growing beneath it. Tulips are well up and awake by February, many alliums are fresh green or glaucous, and Dutch irises may be as much as 6in (15cm) tall.

Some irises actually flower in winter, notably *Iris unguicularis*, better known to many by its former name, *I. stylosa*. Its delicate, mauve blooms seem too fragile to stand up to winter but in the most popular strains ('Walter Butt' is outstandingly generous) they will flower in every mild spell from late October to the end of March. They are ideal to pick in bud and watch opening in a warm room. Since I can remember, we have always had a band of them at the sunny foot of the lower terrace wall (covered in aubrieta), overlooking the upper moat meadow. The plants are congenitally shabby; you need to resign yourself to that.

The other notable winter-flowering iris is the diminutive *Iris histrioides* 'Major', although its blue flowers are quite large for the 3 to 4in (8 to 10 cm) height of the plant. That will often bloom in January, but always by February. Again, it is much less fragile than it appears. Small plants tend to be easily lost sight of, which means lost, in a large garden, but this bulb, entirely dormant from early June, can be fitted in among the crowns of perennials that don't need to be disturbed for years at a time. (It is the same story with snowdrops, crocuses, and winter aconites.) I have established this iris within a colony of *Euphorbia griffithii* 'Fireglow' in the Wall Garden.

— Bridge across winter —

A very different iris is our native *Iris foetidissima*, which is normally found in chalk and limestone woods. It is evergreen (sometimes you wish it weren't), and its flowers are inconspicuous, but its heavy seed pods open in autumn to reveal rows of brilliant orange seeds, and these often remain decorative throughout the winter.

They are a bridge. So are several mahonias. My favorite is *Mahonia lomariifolia*, a rather gawky evergreen shrub which, like all these mahonias, needs regular and quite severe pruning each spring to keep it well furnished (unless you enjoy bare legs, that is; there are different ways of looking at these

Winter sweetness
Curiously, many winter-flowering plants are sweetly scented. None more so than the winter sweet, Chimonanthus praecox *(above), which is deliciously aromatic, not only in its blossom but also in its roots and stems. Flowering from late November to February, it can easily be frosted but a position near to a warm wall negates most of this danger. The summer foliage is coarse. I try not to notice it.*

Handsome shrubs
Among the most valuable of winter-flowering shrubs are the evergreen hybrids between Mahonia japonica *and* M. lomariifolia, *collectively known as* M. × media. *I have two of these: 'Buckland' (left), generally at its best around Christmas and in January; 'Lionel Fortescue' (below), early enough in November to attract hosts of bees.*

No space required
The February-flowering Crocus chrysanthus *'Gipsy Girl' (below) fills a space at the feet of a glaucous-leaved spurge,* Euphorbia nicaeensis.

GROWING
Winter jasmine

The winter-flowering jasmine, *Jasminum nudiflorum*, may have no scent but it is one of the easiest and most obliging of winter-flowering shrubs. Because its habit is lax, it is usually trained against a wall and this can be of any aspect. A pretty severe trim-over after flowering is advisable, otherwise it can become disheveled. On the other hand, when one of its long shoots touches down, it roots immediately, so this is one of the easiest of plants for exchange among friends. Flowering commences as early as November, before its trifoliate leaves have been shed, but by the time a climax has been reached, sometime in December, the twigs are naked.

things). This species has exquisite pinnate foliage, most elegantly sculpted. Its bright yellow flowers in November-December are an asset. The flowers of *M. japonica* are paler and less dense on longer racemes. They have a wonderful lily-of-the-valley fragrance on the air. Flowering may commence as early as autumn but becomes effective only in February.

The hybrids between these two species are known as *Mahonia × media*, and they have produced several famous cultivars such as 'Charity'. The two I grow are 'Lionel Fortescue' and 'Buckland'. The former makes a great display in November and is popular with foraging bees. The latter, whose presentation is a little more modest, is generally at its peak in December or even January, but dates vary from year to year. Unfortunately, these hybrids inherit little or no scent.

Primroses are great bridge builders. Where the woods around us have been coppiced, primroses may be found in bloom during any mild winter spell. It is the same in my borders, where they have self-sown freely. Polyanthus are no less willing, but slugs are their main problem.

Considering that there are few insects around, it is surprising how many winter flowers are scented. My two Chinese witch hazel bushes, *Hamamelis mollis*, were given to my mother 60 years ago. A very little forcing has them flowering for Christmas and they are at their best in the garden in January, never spoiled by frost. Theirs is a spicy scent. So, in a quite different way, is the wintersweet's, *Chimonanthus praecox*. The oldest of our three bushes was a present from a neighbor before I was born. My mother got very bored with it

Giant with frostbite
The enormous, waterside perennial, Gunnera manicata *(far right), with leaves up to 6ft 6in (2m) across, is eventually laid low by frost. We fold its dead leaves over the center of the colony in winter to protect its fat, pink, resting buds.*

———•———

Pink and mauve
The Chinese witch hazel, Hamamelis mollis *(right), with its delicious, spicy scent, can always be gently forced indoors to flower at Christmas. January is its main season, as it is of* Rhododendron dauricum, *which I have planted by its side.*

'Jewel'. Both have lavender flower spikes and a honey-sweet fragrance. Of snowdrops and crocuses, I have probably said enough in my Meadow chapter (see pages 40-47), but some of the *Crocus chrysanthus* strains, notably 'Snow Bunting', are deliciously honey-scented and so are most snowdrops, especially *Galanthus nivalis* itself. I'm trying to get more of these among my *Helleborus orientalis* hybrids. By the time we have cut away the old foliage on these, so that their flowers show up better, there is room for snowdrops between the clumps.

My earliest hellebore to flower, always out by Christmas, is *Helleborus orientalis abchasicus* 'Early Purple'. A pleasing though somber shade of reddish purple, it grows where sunshine never reaches and needs snowdrops to highlight it. My other favorite is our native stinking hellebore, *H. foetidus*. Its evergreen foliage makes such beautiful rosettes, their darkness setting off the lighter green of flowering stems and nodding bells (stained purple around the mouth). Young plants are much the smartest and, because they self-sow very willingly, I ruthlessly ditch third-year plants.

Fruits, bark and seeds

Berries belong to summer and winter as well as to autumn. My 'Golden King' holly (*Ilex* × *altaclerensis*) at the top of the Long Border is the best year-round feature in it (along with *Euonymus fortunei* 'Silver Queen'), but is further enhanced in those years when it is laden with crops of crimson berries. The mistle thrushes sometimes hold off them until after Christmas. The large red *Skimmia japonica* berries seem not to interest the birds. These are borne by female bushes, while the male 'Rubella' makes an interesting contrast with clusters of dormant, dusky red flower buds and reddish leaf margins.

I am proud of my hermaphrodite form of butcher's broom, *Ruscus aculeatus*, which berries freely — large, deep red fruits held through most of the winter. It comes true (though very slowly) from seed, which I was originally sent by an American; he originated his stock from our old Sunningdale Nurseries. So it twice crossed the Atlantic before reaching me. As normally seen, without fruit, the butcher's broom is dull, though it may be useful in deterring people and dogs from taking unwelcome shortcuts through the garden.

Those teazels again

At the time this picture (above) was taken, the canna foliage behind the teazels had still not been frosted, but the skeletons will retain their shapes throughout the winter, taking on a saucy appearance when capped by snow. Their seeds will continue to provide food for goldfinches.

because it just grew (its leaves are coarse and unprepossessing) and never flowered. Until it did! All was then forgiven. Wintersweets are usually raised from seed, and you can have a seedling for six or eight years before it flowers.

Lonicera × *purpusii* is the best of the winter-flowering bush honeysuckles (I also have *L. fragrantissima*, but that holds on to a proportion of its leaves, which is a mistake). Heavily scented white flowers are borne in pairs along all its young shoots. Another group of winter-flowering shrubs with a sickly sweet fragrance (but none the less welcome for that) are the evergreen sarcococcas. I have about five different species of these and would say that the most satisfactory with me as good-looking features are *Sarcococca ruscifolia* and *S. hookeriana digyma*. The latter makes a suckering thicket and needs frequent rejuvenation by cutting old growths right out.

My neighbor just over the fence grows two clones of the January-flowering *Daphne bholua* very well. I don't, but my *D. mezereum* and *D. odora* 'Aureomarginata' are blooming in February with their headachy sweet scents.

Hebes may be a hangover from summer and autumn, but I can often pick 'Midsummer Beauty' in midwinter, and also

Winter bloomers

The hybrids of Helleborus orientalis *(left), also known as Lenten roses, will often be in flower at midwinter, though at their best in February and March. Their fleshy stems collapse during frost, but recover turgidity as soon as the pressure relents. Old leaves look pretty disreputable in my garden, so we cut these away just as the first flowers are opening.*

The clusters of rcd, costume-jewelry berries on my *Aucuba japonica* 'Longifolia' do not ripen until February. It is nice then to have them so fresh.

Many ivies also look good in winter. In the adult bush form of *Hedera helix* 'Poetica Arborea', its clusters of berries are a principal attraction after its October flowering. They ripen to a dusky yellow in February and are immediately set upon and stripped by pigeons. Wood pigeons also love the not-quite-ripe fruit of wild ivy growing up the ash trees on our garden boundaries in February. The clatter of the pigeons' wings as they precariously reach out to grab the fruit while trying to retain their balance always makes me laugh.

Long Border mess
In some respects I am a messy gardener. I don't clear many of the borders until spring. The crocosmia foliage (below) remains good both in color and shape for many months and its attractions are heightened when rimed with frost.

Every gardening journalist, desperate for winter subjects to write about, turns to colorful bark in shrubs and trees. It's not a subject I exactly home in on, but the dogwoods, *Cornus alba*, by the Horse Pond, can be admired twice over in their reflections. Another moisture lover, *Salix alba* 'Britzensis', flourishes in a broken row by the lower moat and I admire it from my bathroom when dressing in the mornings. It is deep orange on its young stems; to encourage plenty of these, we pollard it every second or third year.

Because I do not clear my borders until the spring, skeletons remain, notably of teazels and cardoons, taking on a saucy air when capped by snow. The brown buns that cover the hortensia hydrangeas are decorative, 'Nigra' being especially prolific. Catkins extend on the hazels early in the year, and on the alders soon after. Winter is not a season in which one wishes to linger indefinitely, but there is a feeling of movement throughout and a keen sense of anticipation.

Winter meets spring
The mauve pad of an early-flowering aubrieta, growing in the circular steps, overlapped this common snowdrops's flowering (below). You can pop snowdrop bulbs into all sorts of odd corners that would otherwise be naked in winter but are fully covered by the foliage of neighboring plants in summer.

Capricious iris
Iris reticulata (above) prefers a lighter soil to mine, where its bulbs are generally devoured by slugs.

Bamboos for impact

LIKE SOME of the tallest grasses, bamboos add a feeling of style and presence to a garden. They generally look best standing on their own or, at the least, rising well above any plants surrounding them. Because some bamboos can generate 10 or 12 ft (3 or 3.5m) of growth in a few weeks, this is not too difficult to achieve.

Culturally, bamboos fall into two classes: those that run and those that form fairly stable clumps. You cannot make a firm distinction between these, because in warmer, moister climates, clump-formers will change their style and become runners. In the climate of most of Britain, *Phyllostachys* will generally behave themselves as only moderate spreaders, but I noticed in North Carolina how difficult it was to keep the species separate, in a collection. Well, that's their problem.

The runners among bamboos can, of course, have their uses where a considerable area needs colonizing, and can be spared for their invasive propensities. The only two bamboos I have that sometimes run are both quite dwarf, and they make colonies rather than specimens. Both are arundinarias. I shall give their more familiar names, with the latest thinking on the subject (itself in constant flux) in brackets. The botanists do not make life easy for bamboo enthusiasts.

— Arundinaria colonies —

Arundinaria viridistriata (Pleioblastus auricomus) has leaves striped yellow and green; the color is much its brightest if the entire colony has been shorn to the ground each April. The young canes that then take over are brilliant, and will grow no more than 3ft (1m) tall in a season. *A. variegata (Pleioblastus variegatus)* is in the Barn Garden, hard up against the paving at the border's margin. Its foliage is striped fresh green and white. Sometimes I cut it down, if it has made 3ft (1m) of growth in the previous year; sometimes I leave it for two or three years. It takes several years to settle down entirely, but when growing vigorously is best given an annual cut-back.

Arundinaria variegata can be quite a menacing spreader under border conditions. It will send out long, horizontal rhizomes, a little below the soil surface and invisible in the first year. By the second, when these start sprouting, control will be more difficult. It is wise, I find, to go around my colony every spring, reducing its circumference to where I want it. When it sprouts between the paving cracks, I resort to weedkiller.

The most noticeable bamboo, which you see on your left as you approach the house entrance, replaced a dull ball-and-saucer topiary yew in the center of a lawn. This is the Chilean *Chusquea culeou*. It makes long, dark green brushes of foliage, densely set on closely spaced nodes.

Not unlike the chusquea in its somber coloring and style is *Arundinaria tessellata (Thamnocalamus tessellatus)*, on the brink of the Horse Pond. That is surrounded by a colony of the huge-leaved *Gunnera manicata*. The gunnera is a rhizomatous perennial. Like many such, it continually marches outward, leaving the central area, where it was originally planted, bare. A friend, John Codrington, suggested that the contrast of a bamboo would look good, rising from the center of the gunnera colony. And it does. We thin out the canes of this bamboo every second or third year, leaving only those (still short on leaves) made during the previous summer. Newly pruned, this bamboo looks quite surrealistic.

Another arundinaria of which I am fond and have two clumps is *Arundinaria falconeri (Drepanostachyum falconeri)*. About 7 or 8 ft (2.1 or 2.5m) tall, its canes are thin and flexible, arching over beneath the weight of rain. Raindrops hang silvered on the undersides of these arched canes. But this can be an awkward habit if the bamboo is sited anywhere near a path, giving an unwanted shower bath to swishers-by. Each spring we remove all canes except those of the previous year, and they may have to be tied back, fairly loosely, to a support. But this is one of the most graceful and charming of bamboos. Not quite hardy, but if all its top growth is killed to the ground, it soon returns from the base.

Fast grower
This Arundinaria auricoma (syn. Pleioblastus auricomus), *photographed here in July (above), is cut to the ground annually in April.*

The slim trim
It is good policy with most of the taller bamboos (above), to thin out all their older canes annually or biennially, thus removing clutter that can give an impression of middle-aged obesity. To be able to see right through a colony, and out the other side, is marvelous.

Teazel and bamboo
In close up (left), details from the left page picture, taken in my Long Border. The bamboo is usually pretty well behaved in England's climate but is a great runner where summers are hotter, such as in New England, where it will quickly make a large colony.

Eyecatcher
This Chilean bamboo, Chusquea culeou (above), is the one big feature in front of our house, where it replaced a ball-and-saucer topiary yew. In such a key position, the occupant should draw the eye. This bamboo certainly succeeds in that. Moon daisies have sown themselves at its feet.

— *Phyllostachys merits* —

Most of the rest of my bamboos belong to the genus *Phyllostachys*, and I do find this, by and large, the most satisfactory group. *Phyllostachys* present themselves with pride. Their leaves are a light, bright green, and, although they may look a bit dowdy in spring and early summer, they become radiantly fresh at summer's end and retain this condition into the New Year. Most effectively placed, although I say it, is *Phyllostachys nigra*, 12ft (3.8m) tall and sited

with the dark background of yew, including the big topiary yew tree that preceded the Lloyd's at Dixter. Lutyens' addition to Dixter and, beyond that, the oast house, comprise an architectural background. I have three other varieties of *P. nigra*. The one I have just described came from a colony in Sheffield Park Gardens, 35 miles (56km) away. I particularly liked the smart blackness of its canes. Now that I have it, I find that the canes do not become black until at least three years old, by which time they need removing. I am still looking for a clone in which the canes turn black within a year.

Phyllostachys viridiglaucescens is my most vigorous species. That is in a border in the High Garden and, not surprisingly

Stripy canes

More of a colonizer in our climate than most of the Phyllostachys, *P. bambusoides 'Castillonis' (above) has a bright green stripe on the flat surface of canes that are otherwise yellow.*

Bankside exotics

By the Horse Pond (opposite), giant-leaved Gunnera manicata *marched ever outward, eventually leaving a bare patch in the center of the colony. Into this, for dramatic contrast, I planted the proudly stiff bamboo,* Arundinaria tessellata *(syn.* Thamnocalamus tessellatus). *It seems most appropriate to a pondside setting.*

perhaps, there is a pretty arid area around its base in which other plants are not too keen to grow.

I am establishing two or three in the orchard's meadow turf, which is extremely competitive for nutrients, so we give the bamboos a heavy annual mulch. Even so, I cannot keep them as moist as they would like in the summer. The most exciting of these is *Phyllostachys bambusoides* 'Castillonis'. A distinguishing feature in phyllostachys is the flattened strip running up one side of the cane between the nodes. This flat strip along each internode alternates from one side of the cane to the other, at the interruption of each node. In 'Castillonis', the flat strip on young canes is green, whereas the main cane coloring is yellowish. The contrast is striking.

Being an impulse buyer and acquirer of plants I have to have, I often take on a new bamboo without knowing where I shall find a place to show it off to advantage. I never want them to look like a collection. They must take their place with many other treasures. One of my more recent acquisitions was a green-and-white variegated form of *Phyllostachys aurea*. We have four old brick cattle-drinking tanks, dating back to when the garden was a farmyard, but they have not had water in them since the freeze of 1963. In one, where the Rose Garden now is, I have the giant reed grass, *Arundo donax*, whose presence is similar to a bamboo's. The phyllostachys has been planted in another of these tanks and liberally watered during the summer. My, what growth! I thought variegated plants were weak, but this one is not.

GROWING
Bamboos

It is in our care of bamboos that most of us go wrong. Their individual canes will live for a number of years, in most cases deteriorating steadily from the second year on. All these older canes need thinning out on a regular basis. Take a saw or pruners to them, and make your cuts flush with the ground so as to leave no awkward stumps to be avoided next time the job is to be done. Stumps look bad, anyway. Cane thinning is quite energetic and time-consuming, but how proud you'll be of the result once it is done. The canes that remain now look like tree trunks in a forest, rather than an amorphous thicket. Food and water are the bamboo's other requirements.

Topiary at Dixter

MY FATHER was very keen on the art of topiary – the training and clipping of shrubs into shapes – and there is a lot of it, in yew, at Dixter. There used to be quite a lot more, but much has happened since my father died in 1933. Some specimens grew too big for the scale of their positions. Some died because the ground in which they stood was badly drained. My mother had two archways over flagstone paving removed because flagstones are slippery in wet weather at the best of times; under overhanging branches they develop a patina of algae, making them more dangerous still.

I have never replaced a specimen that died with another, to train in its place. My kind of creativity is not in that direction, and neither is anyone else's here. So the gaps have either been left as gaps or been filled with some other specimen plant that I fancy. But much remains and I enjoy it.

— *Like it or loathe it* —
Many people have strong feelings about topiary. Not long ago I wrote an article about these gardens for an American magazine whose editor disliked topiary. From the photographs taken to illustrate it, he selected many showing the meadow areas, but not one showing the topiary. You'd have thought we had none. The result was strangely unreal. What I like about this garden is the contrasts it presents between geometrically formal and free style.

The area called the Topiary Garden now has five pieces missing. The lawn where they are set was the piece of turf of which my father was proudest, and where he practiced putting, for he was a keen golfer. For my part, I find lawn care a great bore and excessively time-consuming, so this lawn (and not only this one) has been flagrantly neglected, apart from the occasional application of selective herbicide. The grass has formed a dense, fibrous mat, much of it dead, and this has, of course, impeded drainage. That was what upset the missing yews. (We have lately put in some new drains; so you see I am not entirely without conscience.)

In fact, there are beautiful views from the far side of this garden, looking back to the house and Oast House, particularly in the evening light. Topiary has the greatest presence when the shadows are long. The pieces will then seem to people a garden and are excellent company. Good also, of course, when capped with snow, which gives them a rakish look, even more amusing than was the original intention. For topiary was never intended to be taken over-seriously. Those who dislike it are generally lacking in a sense of humor, I find, and seem to feel that their own sense of importance and personal status is under attack.

The Topiary Garden has, on one side, a long-embrasured oak seat, to Lutyens' beautifully simple design, which echoes the structure of the house as you look at it when sitting there. Across the lawn is the hovel, once a cow shed, and when you have walked through that you are in the Rose Garden, which was formerly the cattle yard and still includes one of their original brick drinking tanks.

— *Brilliant design* —
Lutyens' design for this garden, particularly in the scalloped outline of its yew hedging, is brilliant. These hedges are broad-based and solid; flat-topped (whereas in the rest of the garden they are rounded), with buttresses to strong pillars. Yet, because of their sweeping curves, they are elegant. In most of the garden the yew hedges are straight, but, in one other key position, they are allowed a less severe curving, and that is where they meet at the big topiary yew and the yew arch

Enigmatic assembly
Long winter shadows and rime on the grass (above) well suit the gnomic shapes of topiary on the lawn that my father mainly devoted to this feature. If trimmed in early autumn, yews will retain their sharp outline through to late spring.

One of a pair
The yew coffee pots (right) face each other across a path. Because the handle is at right angles to the spout, they should properly be termed French chocolate pots. Yellow Allium moly *has colonized their skirts for the past half-century.*

over the path beneath it. The big yew was the only tree of its kind at Dixter when my parents bought the house in 1910. It was a free-standing specimen. My father trimmed it hard back – a treatment to which yew responds very well – and when it had grown again from its basic structure, he trained it into a conical figure with platforms in the cone. He took photographs of it at all stages in this development, and they are reproduced in his book, *Garden Craftsmanship in Yew and Box*, published in 1925. The view of this yew with the arch and converging hedges (all highly architectural where seen as foreground to Lutyens' wing of the house itself, the projecting porch, and the oasts and barn in the distance) is one of my favorites in the whole garden.

—— *Battered, but unbowed* ——

The reasons why our yew hedges and topiary have a firm, strong, and comfortably settled look are, first, that they were trimmed annually from the year after planting. Many gardeners make the mistake of waiting till a hedge or topiary piece has grown as large as they want it before it sees the shears. This makes for a loose texture easily damaged by snow (or by children barging into it). Second, my father was well aware of how unexpectedly broad a base a hedge requires if it is not to look unbalanced or top heavy, and he allowed for this. Third, he trained all the hedges and most of the topiary plinths on a batter – in other words, sloping inward from the base toward the top. If you make a hedge vertical from the start, the top will receive more light than the base and will grow more strongly, eventually leading to an overhang, which looks weak, not to say stupid.

—— *Variations in color* ——

My father would certainly be shocked if he could see how I have allowed his hedges to bulge and billow, whereas he was so strict about trimming them to exactly horizontal, using a spirit level, and with a perfectly graded batter, for which he designed another guiding instrument. The individual components in a yew hedge are all seedlings; they are seldom raised by the slower and more exacting method of cuttings. Thus they are all genetically different, some more vigorous than others, and with a variation in color that shows up most clearly on the young growth in late spring. I like this variation,

Invitation

Archways in hedges, subdividing different garden areas, invite you to look beyond and to satisfy your curiosity. These two pictures show both sides of the arch. In the High Garden (above), narrow flower borders flank the path and are backed by espalier pears, behind which are plots of vegetables and rows of plants serving the nursery. In what used to be the Lavender Garden (left), but lavender hated our heavy soil, there are now double hedges of a compact Michaelmas daisy, Aster lateriflorus 'Horizontalis', and these link the topiary peacocks, of which there are 18 pieces. In a central group, they face each other across a paved area.

Same peacock, different time
*In April (left), when the daffodils are
at their peak – here you see the
narcissus 'John Evelyn' – the yews are
still severely in their winter garb. The
contrast between severe and the light-
hearted experiences an exchange of
roles when, some six weeks later, the
yews put on a new dress (below).
Their young shoots vary in color from
plant to plant and from light green to
bronze, but their message
is the same; spring has hit them
at last. They can maintain
their severity no longer.*

and I enjoy the way in which the pieces refuse to be pawns in a geometrical game, a hilarious subversion of a too-serious view of what a garden should be.

— *Conversation piece* —

The other area of topiary specimens consists of 18 peacocks perched on pyramidal plinths. At least they are now all re-ferred to as peacocks in their obese old age (though some visitors mistake them for squirrels). Early photographs and the captions in my father's book, however, clearly indicate quite a menagerie of birds, including a blackbird, tail up and looking belligerently territorial, a pheasant, and a pair of fighting cocks daring each other across a path. Ten of these pieces are centrally gathered around a paved area. These my mother sometimes referred to as a "parliament of birds,"

sometimes as a conversation piece. The other eight face each other in pairs and are outliers.

Since 1947 we have used electric trimmers for all topiary and yew-hedge cutting. Originally, the job, started at the ideal moment in August, was completed in six weeks by six men with six hand-shears. Now we never get started until the end of September and the job, executed by Simon, who gives us two days a week, drags on until mid-February. Machinery has helped to compensate for greater labor costs, but it can only do so much. The advantage of an August trim is that no further growth will occur until the end of the following May. The yews will be sharp in outline for nine months, woolly for only three – which, being the summer months when we are most visited, just happens to be the time when they are most frequently photographed!

INDEX

'Torch' *104*, 105
tree lupin *129*
tree mallow, see *Lavatera*
Triteleia laxa 83
Trochodendron aralioides 62
Tropaeolum 'Hermine
  Grashoff'116
  T. majus 105
  T. tricolorum 113, 115
Tulipa 28-33, *28-33*, 64, 112
  T. 'China Pink' *30*, *31*, 32
  T. 'Couleur Cardinal' *28*
  T. 'Estella Rijnveld' *28*, 32
  T. 'Flaming Parrot' *32*, *32*
  T. 'Halcro' *30*, *30*, 33, 67
  T. 'Hollywood' *15*, *28*, 33
  T. 'Magier' *31*
  T. praestans 67
  T. 'Purissima' *30*, *30*
  T. 'Rembrandt' *31*
  T. 'Spring Green' *32*, 33
  T. 'Texas Gold' 28, *32*, *33*

Tulipa 'White Emperor', see
  T. 'Purissima'
  T. 'White Triumphator' 32

U V

Ulmus 'Dampieri Aurea' 25
valerian, see *Centranthus*
Valeriana phu 'Aurea' *15*, 37
Veratrum 19
  V. album 79
Verbascum 54, *69*, 74
  V. bombyciferum 'Arctic
    Summer' 64, *64*
  V. chaixii 59
  V.c. 'Album' *70*, *72*
  V. olympicum 59, 64, *64*, 74
Verbena bonariensis 80, 85
  V. peruviana 116, *117*
  V. tenuisecta 116
vetch, see *Vicia*

Viburnum rhytidophyllum 25
  V. tinus 25
Vicia cracca 44, 48
Vinca difformis 125
  V. minor 125
Viola 'Coeur d'Alsace' 83
  V. odorata 83, *84*
Virginia creeper, see
  Parthenocissus
Viscaria 'Rose Angel' 83, 112

W

wallflower 64, 80, 128; see
  also *Cheiranthus*
  Siberian 64, *67*
wand flower *25;* see
  also *Dierama*
water soldier 98
water violet, see *Hottonia*
waterlily, see *Nymphaea*

Weigela florida 'Variegata' 39
Welsh poppy *10*, *15*, 59, *110;*
  see also *Meconopsis*
willow 97, 99
  bush 17
  silver 19, 57
willow gentian, see *Gentiana*
windflower 101
winter sweet, see
  Chimonanthus
Wisteria sinensis 131
witch hazel, see *Hamamelis*
wood anemone *45*

Y Z

yew 16, *19*, *21*, 23, 25, 152-
  155, *152-155*
Yucca gloriosa 'Nobilis' 61, 79
  Y.g. 'Variegata' *39*, 61, *63*
Zephyranthes candida 123

ACKNOWLEDGMENTS

Steven Wooster and Susan Berry would like to thank Keishi
Colour Ltd. for film processing, and Lynn Bresler for the index.

Dorling Kindersley would like to thank Helen Townsend,
Irene Lyford, Jeanette Mall, and Ray Rogers for editorial
assistance, and Shaun McNally for design assistance.